altered shoes

A STEP-BY-STEP GUIDE TO
MAKING YOUR FOOTWEAR FABULOUS

Marty Stevens-Heebner

altered shoes

A STEP-BY-STEP GUIDE TO
MAKING YOUR FOOTWEAR FABULOUS

Marty Stevens-Heebner

cincinnati, ohio
www.mycraftivity.com
connect. create. explore.

Other fine books from Krause Publications are available from your local bookstore or craft store, or visit us at our web site at www.fwmedia.com.

13 12 11 10 09   5 4 3 2 1

DISTRIBUTED IN CANADA BY FRASER DIRECT
100 Armstrong Avenue
Georgetown, ON, Canada L7G 5S4
Tel: (905) 877-4411

DISTRIBUTED IN THE U.K. AND EUROPE BY DAVID & CHARLES
Brunel House, Newton Abbot, Devon, TQ12 4PU, England
Tel: (+44) 1626 323200, Fax: (+44) 1626 323319
Email: postmaster@davidandcharles.co.uk

DISTRIBUTED IN AUSTRALIA BY CAPRICORN LINK
P.O. Box 704, S. Windsor NSW, 2756 Australia
Tel: (02) 4577-3555

Library of Congress Cataloging in Publication Data
Stevens-Heebner, Marty
  Altered shoes : a step-by-step guide to making your footwear fabulous / Marty Stevens-Heebner. – 1st ed.
       p. cm.
  Includes index.
  ISBN 978-1-60061-126-1 (alk. paper)
  1. Shoes. 2. Fancy work. I. Title.
  TT678.5.S74 2009
  746.4-dc22

Editor: Jennifer Claydon

Cover designer: Wendy Dunning

Interior designer: Rachael Smith

Production coordinator: Matt Wagner

Photographers: Christine Polomsky and Tim Grondin

Photo stylist: Nora Martini

Metric Conversion Chart

To convert	to	multiply by
Inches	Centimeters	2.54
Centimeters	Inches	0.4
Feet	Centimeters	30.5
Centimeters	Feet	0.03
Yards	Meters	0.9
Meters	Yards	1.1

DEDICATION

For all my creative friends and students who inspire me in more ways than they know; for my father, who may not be shoe-obsessed, but who does love anything his daughter designs; and for my late mother, whose charm, grace and color sense will never be forgotten.

ACKNOWLEDGMENTS

I'm eternally grateful to Jay Staten for setting up this book at F + W Media and to my gold-star editor Jennifer Claydon for always being so helpful and clear about what was needed. Thanks also to photographer Christine Polomsky for all of the beautiful pictures in these pages and to keen-eyed Rachael Smith for a vibrant book design. I could never have gotten everything prepped without the help of Rorey Chmielewski, who, along with Jeanne Lusignan and Trudy Rich, is invaluable when it comes to the running of my company.

ABOUT THE AUTHOR

Marty Stevens-Heebner is the president and CEO of Half the Sky Designs LLC and is the creator of the Rebagz™ handbag line. She has appeared on HGTV and the DIY Network and is the coauthor, along with Christine Calla, of *Beading Vintage-Style Jewelry* (Sterling Publishing/Lark Books). Her jewelry and shoe designs have also graced the cover of *Belle Armoire* magazine and been featured in *Belle Armoire's Altered Couture* and *Belle Armoire's Jewelry* magazines. Her Rebagz™ handbags have been featured in dozens of magazines in the U.S. and internationally. You can contact the author at Marty@halftheskydesigns.com and see more of her work at www.halftheskydesigns.com.

contents

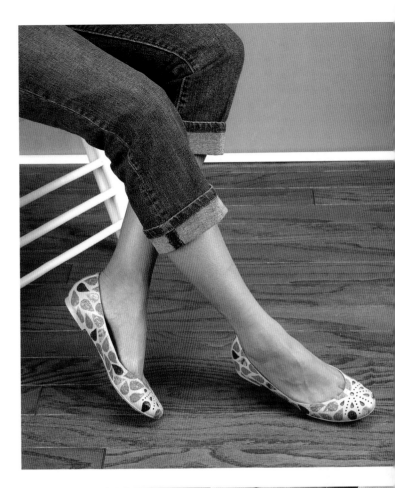

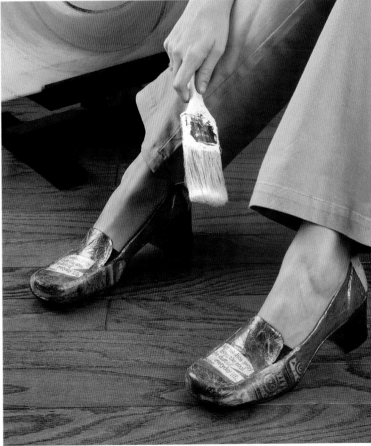

INTRODUCTION

Once upon a time, shoes may have been strictly utilitarian, made simply to keep our feet safe and warm as we walked from one place to another. But time and tastes have evolved to the point where practicality is an afterthought and footwear alone is enough to make a fashion declaration. Until now, you've had to hope that somewhere there's a shoe designer who would miraculously create shoes that mirrored your singular style. Unless your name's Cinderella, however, that probably hasn't happened. Instead, you've been settling for shoes in the right color, of the right height or that simply seemed okay.

Here at last is your chance to be your own shoe designer—or redesigner, as the case may be. Whether you're working with new shoes or ones you've broken in, you'll finally be able to put your own personal stamp on them. Have you found a pair with the perfect shape but a horrible color? Change it! Heading for a party and want to make sure your shoes shimmer while you dance? It's easy to add sparkle to your stilettos to better catch the light when you kick up your heels. This book is here to show you how.

Doesn't it just break your heart when your most beloved shoes get scuffed, torn or otherwise maimed? They've been such good friends to you, carrying you on your way, that it seems horrible to abandon them now. In this case, you get to be both designer and rescuer. Don't cast them aside—transform them instead! That way, you get the best of both worlds: shoes with a delicious new design without the usual new-shoe blisters.

Maybe you've never set foot in a craft store. Maybe you have enough glue guns and glue sticks for an entire army of fashionistas. Wherever you stand on the crafting spectrum, you'll find projects in these pages to suit your experience level, as well as plenty of instructions and inspiration to guide you along your way. Take a stroll through these pages and you'll discover techniques for working with paint, gilding and polymer clay. Renew your shoes using one idea or several. All of the design decisions are entirely up to you.

Your feet carry you on your journey through life. So why shouldn't a book on altered shoes forge a new creative path for you? Whatever you do—whether you're saving a tired but favorite pair of flats, improving a pair of new black pumps or turning those bridesmaid shoes into something wearable now that the wedding's over—above all be daring. Create something that doesn't just go with your outfit but punctuates it. Do something that makes people look, that lets them know you truly have a style all your own.

It's time to create your own footwear fairy tale. Now when you step out in your latest open-toed fabrication and someone asks you, "Where'd you get those shoes?" you'll get to say, "I designed them," and watch their jawbones hit the floor. Congratulations—you've just declared your fashion independence!

Materials

When it comes to the options for making your footwear fabulous, the only limitation is size. The embellishments you choose should more or less fit on the shoe itself and shouldn't be too heavy, or you'll find yourself dragging around feet that feel like lead. Beyond that, the choices are endless. There are the obvious picks—rhinestones, paper, fabric and ribbon—and the more unusual ones—metallic leaf, stray jewelry pieces and small leftover holiday decorations. When picking out embellishments, consider how you'll wear the shoes. Will they be just for special occasions, or do you plan on stomping all around town in your new creations? For shoes that need to last, choose embellishments that can take some pounding. Want real inspiration? Check out your "miscellaneous" drawer—you're likely to find something surprising and fun.

SHOES TO BE ALTERED

Picking a pair of shoes to transform is actually very easy because you can work with just about any new or used shoes, boots, sneakers or sandals. You can even put two different shoes together, as long as the shape and size are similar. But there are a few things to keep in mind when choosing a pair to play with.

If you elect to alter new shoes, choose inexpensive ones. Why pay designer prices for a pair you're going to redesign yourself? Go bargain hunting instead. Hit the sales, outlet stores and thrift shops. You can snag some great deals online, but be sure your cyberstore has a good return policy in case the shoes don't fit properly. Remember that sizes can vary between brands.

There's another thing to bear in mind regarding size: A bit of shrinkage can occur during the design process. It doesn't always happen, but it's something to consider, especially if you're working with new shoes. If you're simply attaching a few small embellishments, you won't need to worry; if you're decoupaging the entire shoe or otherwise completely covering it, there's a good chance it will feel less flexible. That doesn't necessarily mean you should buy a bigger shoe size, but if the shoes feel tight before their makeover, you should opt for a slightly larger pair.

I must admit my favorite shoes to work with are the used ones I've banished to the back of my closet due to damage or a severe lack of style. Granted, if the entire heel's separated from the shoe or if there's a tear completely through the body, then a trip to the shoe repair shop is required. But cosmetic cover-ups are easy. How many times have you had to quit wearing your favorite pair of shoes because you've tripped and scuffed the side of one of them? I'm sure to get a heel torn up in a subway grate if there's one nearby. Fortunately, these aggravations don't have to mean the end of a shoe's life anymore. Now all it takes is a bit of creative camouflage to save the day.

I've found that bridesmaid shoes and other dyed-to-match pumps are particularly in need of renovation because, while they may be colorful, they're also useless after that one special occasion. Why not get the girls together after the wedding and have a shoe makeover party? Comfort shoes, though noble and kind to the feet, also call out for a boost because they're usually deadly dull. These shoes are really blank canvases waiting for you to exercise your creativity.

Much as we all hate to admit it, we do occasionally get caught up in a fad or two. Somewhere in our closets or under our beds sleep those trendy shoes we just couldn't resist buying. They were all the rage, and now they're as stale as a loaf of last year's bread. Consider this your chance to do the shoe's original designer one better and create stilettos that are timeless instead of fashion trash.

Before you begin to alter your absolute favorite pair of shoes—the ones that are still in good condition and that you wear all the time—do yourself a favor and wait a bit. Don't get carried away and change shoes that you already adore. Know that at some future time they'll need your help. But for now find other shoes, either in your closet or at a nearby store, that cry out for reinvention. Believe me, there are plenty of them out there.

ADHESIVES

Glue is the invisible component that will hold your creations together. It's important to figure out which adhesive will work best with your materials before you begin executing your design so you don't wind up with a sticky mess instead of a sleek new shoe design. While there are many kinds of adhesive to choose from, there are a few basic types that, in my experience, work best for altering shoes.

The adhesive we have all been familiar with since kindergarten is white craft glue. It's very versatile, not too thick, and it dries clear. I've used this on a number of my own projects, especially when I'm dealing with shoes made of fabric or when I'm decoupaging paper onto a shoe. The shoes remain fairly flexible after the glue dries, and white craft glue brushed over the top layer of a design serves as a water-repellent sealant.

For gluing fabric on top of a shoe, rubber cement has proven to be my best choice, especially when I don't plan on sealing the outside of the fabric. First, I spread the rubber cement onto the shoe and let it dry for a bit, then I add the fabric on top of it. This way, the glue doesn't soak through and ruin the sheen of the fabric. If you like the texture of a paper embellishment you're incorporating, rubber cement is probably your best adhesive choice.

Fabric glue is another option, and it certainly will adhere fabric to shoes or any other object. But I've found it to be very thick and messy to work with, and after it dries it can be both inflexible and heavy. However, you may find it worth some experimenting, depending on your designs and materials.

Finally, what list of adhesives would be complete without hot glue and its partner, the glue gun? A hot glue gun is ideal for securely attaching rhinestones, chains, ribbons and other small trinkets to shoes. Just watch your fingers to avoid burns when you're using it.

Before you begin gluing anything onto your pair of shoes, please take the time to test different adhesives to see which seems the most appropriate for the project and is the most comfortable for you to work with. You want to feel confident once that glue starts setting.

PAINT

Few things have more impact on a design than a simple coat of paint. Even a few dabs of color can take your shoes from drab to dynamic with very little time and effort, and paint can be very forgiving. Make a mistake? You can usually just paint over it and start again.

I use water-based acrylic paint most often because it cleans up as easily as it goes on, making it very user friendly. Acrylic paints brush on smoothly and also mix together well if you want to create a customized color. The painted surface remains flexible after it dries, and touch-ups, if necessary, are simple to do. I often like to create a color wash by mixing acrylic paint with water. When used on shoelaces, fabric, lace or over another paint color, a color wash adds a subtle tint or, if you're using a metallic paint, a gentle gleam.

Oil-based paints also add vivid color, but I avoid using them because of the toxic fumes and the difficult cleanup. If you do choose to work with this kind of paint, make sure you use it in an open, well-ventilated area because those vapors can overwhelm you very quickly. You should also keep pets and small children out of the way so your little sweethearts don't get sick

from the fumes. For cleanup, use turpentine or a strong cleaner made specifically for the task, including one for brushes, or you may find yourself tossing out your paintbrushes along with your empty paint cans.

Spray paint also requires proper ventilation, but there are no brushes to clean afterwards and you can get a lot of coverage quickly and easily. Spray painting's pretty basic: Lay down a drop cloth, plant your shoes in the middle, and spray. Just make sure you cover each shoe's entire surface area. It's easy to miss a spot or two, so check thoroughly before tucking the can away.

There are many paints and markers that have been specially designed for use on fabric, although, as noted above, I sometimes work with acrylic paints on cloth. Fabric paints are often thicker in consistency and require more time to dry completely, so read the manufacturer's instructions when you use them. Fabric markers are great fun because it's easy to draw line designs or write phrases, things that are more difficult to do with regular paints. As with fabric paints, follow the manufacturer's instructions, as some fabric markers require heat setting to make them colorfast.

Fabric

Renewing your shoes is a fantastic way to use up scraps of fabric left over from other projects, particularly if you enjoy quilting or sewing. It's great fun to mix and match different fabric designs, and adding cloth to your shoes is actually quite easy. Plus, if you make your own clothes, you can create shoes to go with your new attire. You can be absolutely sure no one else will have an outfit so thoroughly complementary as yours.

Just about any fabric will work on a shoe, though heavy cloth, like thick corduroy, may not mold easily to the shoe and will probably fray quite a bit. Lightweight fabrics, such as thin cotton or silk, work well, but make sure the glue you choose doesn't soak through, unless you want a slightly transparent effect. Mixing heavy and lightweight fabrics in the same shoe design can create an awkward look, but if you separate the different materials with a bit of trim, you can get away with just about anything.

You can cut fabric in a free-form style, as in the *Crazy Quilt Granny Boots* on page 54, or you can cut fabric to match the shape of the shoe, like I did with the *Stamp Your Foot Loafers* on page 76. Following the shape of the shoe creates a more precise look, while free-form style usually results in something more casual or flamboyant.

Layering a translucent fabric over another fabric is definitely something worth experimenting with. The top piece should complement the cloth design underneath, and it can even help tone down a too-vivid pattern that might otherwise be overpowering, no matter how much you love it. You can also use lace very effectively in this manner, particularly if your style has a romantic or vintage feel.

One of the most important things you should do before dismissing any fabric is to examine its reverse side. I've often bought fabric because I liked the back of it rather than the front. You'll be amazed how attractive the so-called wrong side can be!

paper

Colored paper, rice paper, newspaper, wrapping paper—paper's everywhere, and you can have so much fun with it. You can clip it precisely or rip and shred it; it all depends on what you're in the mood to create. In this book you'll find designs that incorporate these kinds of paper and others as well, like photos, maps, playing cards and sheet music.

Like paint, paper is an easy way to add vibrant color to your footwear. Like fabric, paper with a printed design can add an intricate pattern to your shoes. And, just like translucent fabric can be layered over another fabric, tissue paper can be added over another paper, paint or fabric for a translucent effect.

Different thicknesses of paper need to be handled in different ways. Thin, fragile papers, like tissue paper or newspaper, can tear easily, especially when wet, and need to be handled with care. (Should you tear it by accident, carefully lay the pieces down next to one another and brush glue over the tear; you'll more than likely be the only one to notice it.) Thick paper, on the other hand, can be clumsy if you're trying to mold it around your shoe. An easy way to get any paper to

cooperate is to first soak it in water. Give it a quick bath lasting anywhere from five to forty-five seconds, just long enough for it to become limp and pliable, and you'll be able to bend the paper to your will.

If you decide to work with something you've printed on paper, make sure it won't run or smear. If you're using a laser printer, you shouldn't experience running or smearing, but soaking an image from an ink-jet printer in water is not a good idea. Instead, gently dab glue on top of the image in order to seal it. In fact, using sealant such as white craft glue on paper is good practice so that dirt doesn't get embedded in it. It's also less likely to tear that way.

Once your paper and glue dry, you can add even more color in a couple of ways. As I mentioned earlier, you can mix a little bit of paint in some water to create a color wash and then brush a lot or a little of it over the paper, depending on the effect you're seeking (see *Paint*, page 13). If you're working with a black-and-white image or design, you can color it in using markers, paints or even colored pencils.

embellishments

Let's face it: Shiny things captivate us. Gemstones, neon lights and the stars themselves are so fascinating, it's no wonder we love to create our own things that shimmer. Of course, not all embellishments gleam, but they do all add that special something to a design.

When it comes to adding sparkle, nothing outshines rhinestones and sequins. Their sole purpose is to light up a room, or at least the shoes you're wearing as you cross the floor. These pieces come in all sorts of colors, sizes and shapes, and thanks to every crafter's best friend—the hot glue gun—they're incredibly easy to affix. Small crystals have a similar twinkle, especially if they're faceted, and are just as easy to work with whether they're natural crystals or something more polished, like Swarovski's famous crystals and beads.

Speaking of beads, what about all those castoffs loitering at the bottom of your jewelry box? Broken earrings, necklaces and chains are all treasures that deserve a second life. Next time a bracelet comes apart, instead of cursing its broken clasp, save all the beads, trinkets and charms for some future project. Or head to the bead store with your shoes in mind to see what catches your eye.

Your sewing basket is another place worth mining, particularly if you have lots of colorful buttons waiting for somewhere to belong. It doesn't matter if you have an odd number, since there's no reason your design has to be perfectly symmetrical. Use a single button or stack them on top of each other to add dimension and color.

Have you ever made your own buttons or beads from polymer clay? If you haven't, it's about time you tried. It's a wonderful way to combine the colors you're using into an embellishment that perfectly complements what you already have in place.

Back to your sewing basket: There's bound to be extra bits of trim and spools of ribbon in there, too. I must make a confession here: Trim and ribbon have saved so many of my designs—shoe and otherwise—that I keep extra spools of them lying around just for rescue purposes. They conceal rough edges and provide an easy way to add color contrast to a dull palette. Using trim or ribbon to encircle the shoe where the upper meets the sole gives a particularly finished look. Strips of lace add grace as well as color and camouflage, though you'll have to handle lace more delicately than ribbon.

To truly put your own stamp on your shoe design, why not do so literally? Visit the stamping section of your favorite craft store. The hardest part will be choosing which stamps to use. Their images range from simple to intricate, from elegant to fun. Want to make a statement? Pick a stamp containing a phrase you like, or use letter stamps to spell out what you want to say. Stamps are very easy to work with as long as you remember to let the ink dry thoroughly after you've made your imprint. This rule applies whether you're stamping on paper first or bravely stamping straight onto the shoe.

Like stamps, stickers are available in endless variety. They are especially fun for kids to work with. All you have to do is press the stickers on, and you're ready to step out the door. They're not very durable, though, so keep some extra ones standing by for instant repair. For stickers that last, add a sealant over the top and keep the kids occupied until it's dried thoroughly.

Why not add some memorabilia or everyday objects to your repertoire? Postage stamps, old theater tickets and playing cards all work wonderfully as long as they're not too thick; if necessary you can cut them into pieces

that adhere easily to a shoe. Old passport pages—ones where the visa has expired, that is—also create quite an impact and will remind you of the exotic places you have visited.

There are a few other possibilities that, though very ephemeral, can add a lot of impact. Feathers may only last through one party, but no one will forget them—and you can always replace the withered ones with fresh fluff for the next occasion. Seashells and small holiday ornaments are fragile, but both embody their respective seasons too perfectly to ignore.

Though this list of embellishments may seem extensive, I assure you that as you pursue your own shoe endeavors you'll find yourself adding to it. We've all heard the saying, "If the shoe fits, wear it." In this case, if it'll fit on the shoe, glue it—and if it can't be glued on, just take inspiration from it.

DESIGN AND INSPIRATION

So you've scrutinized the shoes in your closet or the nearest shoe store, then scoured your own crafting provisions along with those at the neighborhood craft store—and now your mind's about to sink from the weight of all the possibilities before you. Fear not! For one thing, who says you have to renew just one pair of shoes? More importantly, remember that creative time is playtime, which means you've been given full license to experiment with any and all crazy ideas. Let your mind roam and your imagination wander. Take a little mental vacation each time you contemplate shoes to renew. You can play in the sand first, dreaming of salty sea breezes and warm sand between your toes, then shift to New York during Fashion Week and imagine strutting down Fifth Avenue in your favorite stilettos. It's just a good idea, while you're conjuring up ideas, to hold off on the glue until you've decided where your design will land.

The first choice you should usually make is which pair of shoes to work with. You can always change your mind, of course, but often the initial inspiration will come from the style of the shoe. Are you thinking about lean sandals with small straps or calf-high boots with thick heels? The little straps mean a small surface to cover, while the boots have room for your design to sprawl out. Then again, maybe you'd like to attach huge flowers to the sandals to draw more attention to them, or decorate only a portion of each boot for something subtle.

The shoe's surface needs to be taken into account, too, though not in a way that should inhibit your decision making. For example, you should simply remember that a slick shoe surface will mean you should sand it a bit so that things will adhere to it. If you're working on a canvas shoe with paint, you'll have to add more than one coat because the material will drink up lots of color. Each type of shoe has different possibilities, so decide early on whether to think big visual impact or small.

Looking for inspiration? We need it when we have too many ideas as well as too few, since inspiration will help generate a focus. Inspiration is closer than you realize. Look to your own memories and your own experiences for ideas. Did you wear the shoes you've chosen on a very special occasion that you'd like to commemorate, or are they left over from one you'd like to paint over and forget? Have you always been a fan of Picasso's "blue period" or did you like that Egyptian exhibit at the museum? Granted, these are notions from a far corner of left field, but didn't they all conjure up some mental image for you?

Themes are a wonderful way to guide your design, whether you're leaning towards something neo-classical or you just like stuff that's yellow. My *Safari Sneakers* on page 120 pay tribute to a trip to Africa I took with my father shortly after my mother died. I've always loved Christmas and I adore the color red, hence my *Santa Baby Stilettos* on page 108. Your ideas can be mundane or highfalutin. All that matters is that you are happy with the result.

Those *Santa Baby Stilettos*, by the way, came to be in an unusual way. Obviously, the small red Christmas ornaments weren't difficult to find. But the golden leaves and sprigs were actually part of one decoration that I deconstructed—which is a nice way of saying I (neatly) tore it apart. There's something very fun and naughty about taking something apart, especially when you have a reason for doing so. The gold decoration I started out with was too cumbersome for the shoe, so I snipped off the back of it and divided it into its separate elements. As a whole, the decoration was useless to me, but the different components were exactly what I needed. So before dismissing something entirely, take time to consider its individual parts in case one of them is just what you're looking for.

If themes seem daunting or unnecessary, simply find a piece of cloth or paper you like and let that lead the

way. Frequently that's how I begin, and, truth be told, my design's so-called theme is often an afterthought. The color and texture of the material you choose will influence what you choose next. Likewise, a stamp or loose pendant can be the compass for your design, though your true North Star should be your own taste.

Sometimes the surest way to learn how to trust your own creative instincts is to invite a bunch of friends over for a shoe-renewing party. Do not—I repeat, do not—invite anyone intent on inflicting their own style on others. Rather, surround yourself with those who celebrate differences, who prefer to laugh rather than issue judgments. Tell them to bring a pair of shoes they no longer wear and to bring any crafting implements they like. The only rule for a shoe-renewing party is that when someone, particularly you, says, "Is this OK? Do you like this?" because they're unsure of themselves, the only response is, "Do *you* like it?" I do this in the classes I teach; while initially my students glare at me, in the end everyone creates something they truly like and that is true to their individual tastes.

Another thing I tell people is that the first thing to do upon making a mistake is to celebrate—that's the mark of a real artist! Consider that many wonderful discoveries happened because of mistakes; stop and examine what you've done, because it may actually trigger a more exciting design. Don't be surprised if your design wanders down a few different avenues before finding its way. Any artist, including this one, can tell you about the different permutations each project had before a final plan was settled on and about accidents and mistakes that turned out to be advantageous rather than disastrous.

Inspiration is everywhere, but most of all it lies within. Instead of fretting over all the choices and decisions before you, make merry with them. Take your time and enjoy what you're doing the same way you'd enjoy a day at the beach or a dinner with your best friend. Give yourself the permission you need to be creative and, most importantly, to have fun.

I used to look at handcrafted things like they were artifacts from another planet—surely it took some unearthly ability to put them together. But, as you shall see, basic crafting techniques are very straightforward and easy to master. The skills I've included here cover all you need to know in order to put together the projects in this book. Using the right method not only makes the project flow better, but it also makes your designs last longer. Knowing what you're doing will also increase your confidence—and that confidence will fire up your imagination.

PREPARING SHOES FOR ALTERING

Before you begin doing anything crafty with your shoes, make sure they're ready for you. A few simple steps is all it takes to pave the road to success. Take my word for it: good preparation always makes a project easier.

1 Sand shoes
Shoes with slick surfaces, such as patent leather, need to be roughed up to give paint or glue something to grab onto. Lightly sand the surface with fine-grit sandpaper.

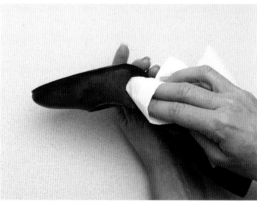

2 Clean surfaces
With a damp cloth, wipe any dirt or sanding residue from the shoes. Allow all surfaces to dry completely.

3 Prime surfaces (optional)
If the shoes you are altering are a dark color and you don't want the original color to show through, prime the shoes with white acrylic paint. Allow the paint to dry completely before proceeding. Some materials, such as canvas, will soak up the first coat of paint you apply, so add a second coat if necessary to completely cover the original color.

PAINTING

With so many types of paint to choose from, how will you decide which one is the best to use for those shoes sitting in front of you? It really depends on what kind of effect you want to create. Do you just want to cover an area with color, or are you looking to do something finer and more precise? What surface will you paint? Ask yourself these questions when you're standing in your craft store's paint aisle, and that will help you to narrow all those choices down considerably.

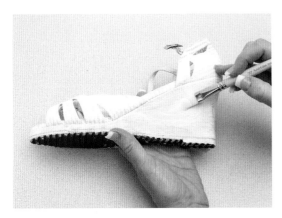

Acrylic Paint

Use acrylic paint to cover large areas or to paint precisely using a fine-tipped brush. Acrylic paint is easy to work with because it provides terrific color and coverage, and when you're done, it cleans up easily with soap and water.

To use acrylic paint, apply paint in an even layer with a paintbrush and allow it to dry completely. Apply additional coats until you get the coverage and hue you want.

Detail Paint

You need a fine-tipped brush to add painted details to your design. This technique is very effective for highlighting small details on shoes that would otherwise go unnoticed.

Choose a brush that is an appropriate size for the design you are painting. As you paint, be patient and work neatly, because it can be tricky to fix mistakes.

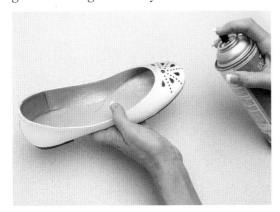

Spray Paint

Spray paint is the perfect way to cover an entire shoe in one color. Work in a well-ventilated area, and use a drop cloth to catch overspray.

Apply paint in an even layer, and allow it to dry completely. Apply additional coats until the color and coverage are as you want them.

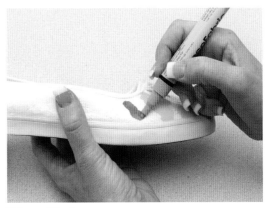

Fabric Markers

Fabric markers are perfect for canvas shoes, especially if you want to add details or cover just a small area.

Decorate the shoes with fabric markers as desired, then follow the manufacturer's instructions to permanently set the design.

CREATING a PATTERN

When you sew a piece of clothing, you use a pattern that provides you with the garment's individual components so you can make it fit precisely. Take a look at your shoes, and you'll see they're put together using different pieces, just like clothes are. Creating pattern pieces to match the different components of your shoes will help you follow their contours more accurately. Sometimes we like to color inside the lines, and this will make it easy for you to do just that.

1 Trace pattern
Lay tissue paper over the part of the shoe that requires a pattern. Using a felt-tip pen or marker, trace on the tissue paper slightly outside the outline of the piece.

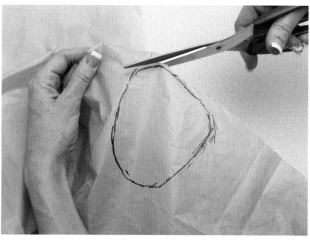

2 Cut tissue paper
Cut the tissue paper slightly outside the traced lines so that the pattern is larger than the piece it is modeled after.

3 Compare pattern to shoe
Lay the cut piece back over the part of the shoe you are making a pattern for, then trim the pattern piece so that it matches the shoe exactly.

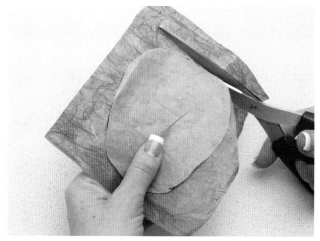

4 Cut final piece
Hold the pattern together with the decorative paper or fabric you will use to cover the shoe. Trim the decorative paper or fabric to the same size as the pattern. Don't mark the pattern on the paper or fabric—unless you want to end up with marks on your finished piece.

DeCOUPAGING WITH PAPER

The word *decoupage* comes from the French verb meaning "to cut," and this technique is all about cutting and pasting. You can cut the paper to fit a part of your shoe exactly, or you can rip it into pieces to create a more carefree design. This means that tearing isn't always a bad thing—you can always claim it was a design choice! But if you're using paper that has a design on it, handle it with care to avoid accidentally shredding that pattern. It's also important to make sure your paper design is sealed so it won't get torn, dirty or ruined by water while you wear the shoes.

1 Apply glue
Select the materials you will work with. If the paper or patterns need to be oriented a certain way, decide how you'll place them before beginning. Apply glue to only the area you are about to cover. Do not coat the whole shoe at once, or the glue may dry before you finish adding the paper.

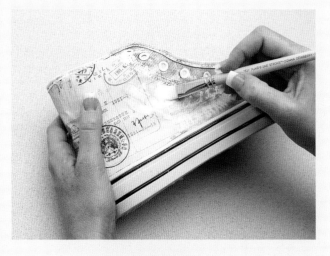

2 Wet paper (optional)
If you are working with thick paper, wet it before adhering it to help make the paper more flexible and easy to shape to the shoe. A quick dip in water to dampen it will suffice.

3 Attach paper
Lay the paper over the glue-covered area. Gently smooth the paper flat. Be very careful when working with wet paper; it can tear easily.

4 Seal paper
Before the bottom layer of glue dries, cover the paper with a thin layer of glue. This will secure the paper more thoroughly to the shoe and prevent dirt from ruining it.

5 Trim paper
After the glue dries, use a craft knife to trim any excess paper away from the edges of the design.

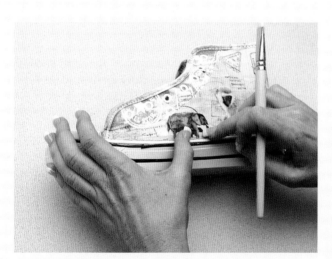

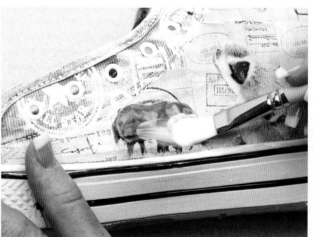

6 Attach second layer of paper (optional)
A second layer of paper can be added to further embellish the shoe. If you'd like a second layer, repeat Steps 1–3 with the new layer of paper.

7 Seal second layer
Seal the second layer of paper to the first with a light coating of glue.

DECOUPAGING WITH FABRIC

While decoupaging with fabric is similar to the process used for paper, there are a few differences. For one thing, fabric frays. You may want some ragged ends to show, but you should seal those stray ends so they won't snag or catch on something—which could not only ruin your shoe design but could also cause a nasty tumble. You'll also need to shape fabric to the shoe more carefully than you do with paper, since fabric doesn't have as much give as paper.

Darts

Just as in sewing, sometimes you need to create a dart in a piece of fabric in order to make it fit your shoe properly. Snip the fabric right where the dart needs to go and remove the extra fabric, just as you do when making a piece of clothing. Unlike sewing, however, you then glue one flap over the other to fit the shoe's contour.

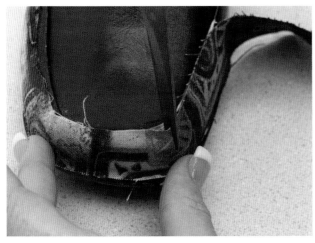

1 Snip fabric
Adhere the fabric to the shoe up to the point where the shoe curves. Snip the fabric directly over the curve.

2 Adhere fabric
Adhere the first part of the snipped fabric to the shoe. Carefully overlap the first part of the snipped fabric with the second to fit the fabric to the shoe.

Tips, Tricks & Crazy Things to Try

Keep a pair of small scissors nearby when working with fabric so you can trim the fabric once you've glued it to the shoe. This is the best way to tame those small threads that emerge from the fabric's edges. A small set of scissors can easily sneak into crevasses and move nimbly around curves to snip off stray threads as well as any excess cloth. Once the glue used to attach the fabric dries, the frayed threads are easy to snip away.

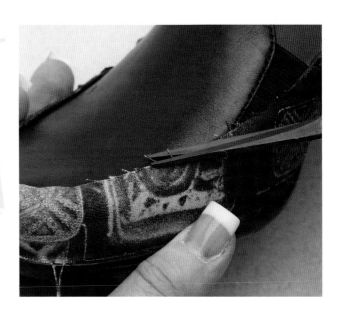

ADDING Trim

Nothing tidies up your edges quite like adding a bit of ribbon or trim. Whether you're confronted with two pieces of paper that didn't quite meet the way they were supposed to or cloth ends that are coming undone, gluing trim over the top will accentuate the shape as well as disguise these gaffes. Even if everything looks perfect, trim can add a terrific dash of color that either complements what you already have or provides needed contrast to a design that would otherwise be drab and dull. Just be sure you seal the ends so they don't unravel while you're out for a stroll.

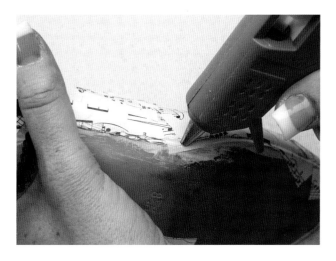

1 Apply glue
Using a hot glue gun, apply a line of glue to the area to be trimmed. For best results, glue down only a few inches of trim at a time.

2 Adhere trim
Press the trim onto the glue, and hold the trim in place until the glue sets.

3 Cut to fit
Adhere the trim to within ½" (1cm) of the place where the trim will end or meet another piece of trim. Carefully measure and cut the trim to fit together seamlessly. Adhere the last ½" (1cm) of trim.

EMBELLISHING WITH RHINESTONES AND BEADS

For the biggest possible "Wow!" rhinestones and beads are the way to go. They can be big and flamboyant or small and shimmering. No matter the size, they always dazzle the eye. They couldn't be easier to work with: Pull your hot glue gun out of its holster and fire away— just plan out your design in advance. You can use rhinestones and beads alone or add them on top of fabric, paper or any other material—even trim or lace.

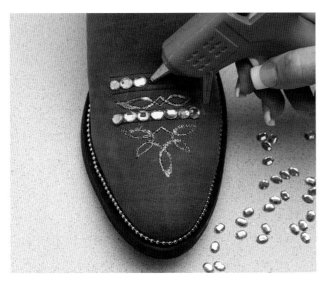

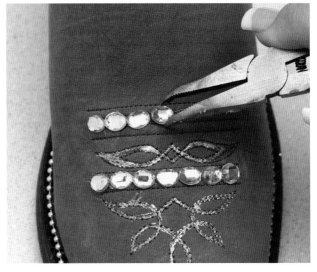

1 Apply glue
I recommend using a hot glue gun to attach rhinestones. Add a very small dab of glue to the shoe where you want to add the rhinestone. Be very careful when applying the glue, because excess glue can mar a shoe's appearance.

2 Adhere rhinestone
Press the rhinestone into the hot glue. Use a pair of tweezers or bent-nose pliers to handle the rhinestone with precision and to save your fingertips from glue burns. Hold the rhinestone in place until the glue is set.

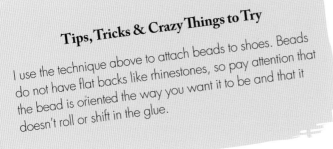

Tips, Tricks & Crazy Things to Try
I use the technique above to attach beads to shoes. Beads do not have flat backs like rhinestones, so pay attention that the bead is oriented the way you want it to be and that it doesn't roll or shift in the glue.

STAMPING

Make your mark with a stamp and ink if you want a truly distinctive design. If you're making a series of imprints or writing a word or phrase using individual letters, experiment with your spacing on a separate piece of paper first. That way, you'll avoid misprints. Be sure to seal the stamp so it won't smear or bleed should you get caught in the rain.

Stamping on Paper

Incorporating a stamp on a piece of paper instead of stamping directly on a shoe can save time and frustration. It can be difficult to use a flat stamp on a curved shoe and get a complete imprint. If your shoes have a smooth, slick surface, it's doubtful the ink will completely adhere to it.

Stamping on a Shoe

If the upper of your shoe is made of a plain, pale canvas, you should be able to stamp directly onto the shoe, but you have to be extremely careful because you only have one shot at making the perfect stamp.

1 Stamp paper
Cut the paper to fit the shoe. It is very important to cut the paper to fit first because that allows you to accurately place the stamped image. (It is much harder to cut paper to size when you are worried about keeping an image centered.) Apply ink to the stamp. Stamp the paper, and allow the ink to dry completely.

1 Stamp shoe
Apply ink or paint to a stamp. To apply paint, use a small paintbrush. Press the stamp firmly onto the shoe, and roll the stamp off cleanly.

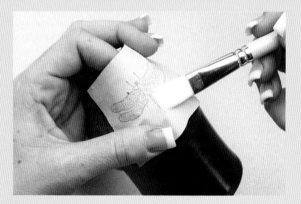

2 Adhere stamped paper
Decoupage the stamped paper to the shoe (see *Decoupaging with Paper*, page 25).

2 Fill in stamp
Stamping directly onto a shoe rarely provides a perfect image. Fill in any imperfections with a small paintbrush.

USING IRON-ON TRANSFERS

If you want to use a photo in your shoe design, iron-on transfers will make that image clear for all to see. Though the process may seem daunting if you've never tried it before, it's really not difficult at all. Whereas paper photos can tear while you're working with them, an iron-on transfer will stay in one piece as you put it in place. Having the photo or image on cloth also seems to add greater dimension to it, perhaps because the ink seeps into the threads as you iron the picture onto the fabric.

1 Print image
Following the manufacturer's instructions, print the image onto iron-on transfer paper. Trim away the excess paper around the image.

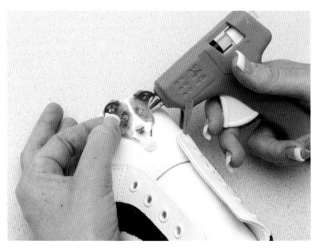

2 Transfer image
Following the manufacturer's instructions, transfer the image to the fabric.

3 Check image
Check the fabric to make sure you are satisfied with the transfer. During the transfer process, the image will be reversed. Take this into account if you plan to transfer an image that contains writing.

4 Adhere image
Trim around the transferred image if you'd like, and then attach the image to the shoe with hot glue.

CREATING POLYMER CLAY EMBELLISHMENTS

If you haven't yet worked with polymer clay, now is the time to try it. It only *seems* like you need a plethora of gadgets to get the clay to do anything. Honestly, I used what I had lying around the house for my *Pumped-Up Polka Dot Stilettos* on page 72. All it took was wax paper, a rolling pin and a razor blade—even a glass bottle would do to flatten the clay. The colors available are so vibrant and the clay itself is so easy to work with that you now officially have no excuse not to play with clay the way you did as a kid.

1 Create clay embellishments
Cut and shape polymer clay into the shape you want. Follow the manufacturer's instructions to bake the clay.

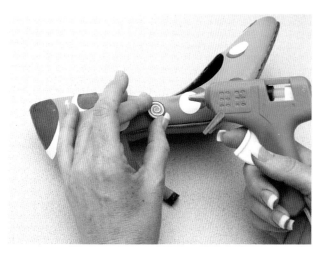

2 Attach clay embellishments
Attach the polymer clay embellishments to the shoe with a hot glue gun.

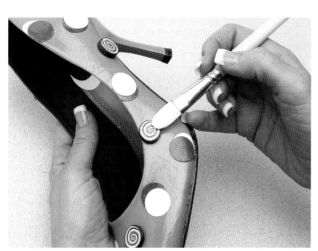

3 Seal clay embellishments
Be sure to seal the clay embellishments. A glossy sealant highlights the clay pieces beautifully.

MAKING WIRE EMBELLISHMENTS

Wire wrapping is another technique that appears complicated but isn't. All it takes is some practice. I compare it to learning a new dance step: The first few times you try it you feel clumsy, but soon you get the feel of it, and then you glide along. Your hand muscles just need to get accustomed to the moves. Once they do, you'll be able to make all kinds of shapes out of wire that are remarkable not only for their form but also for the way they shimmer.

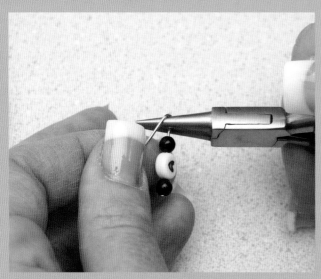

1 **Begin loop**
Slide beads onto a head pin or a piece of wire. Begin to form a loop at the end of the head pin or wire with round-nose pliers.

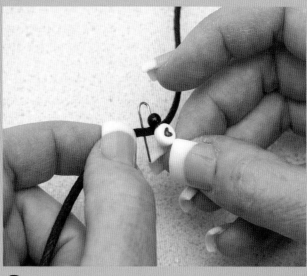

2 **Attach loop**
Before the loop is fully formed, hook the wire around the item it's meant for, such as chain or a shoelace.

3 **Finish loop**
Continue bending the wire to form a full loop. Trim the excess wire so it's flush.

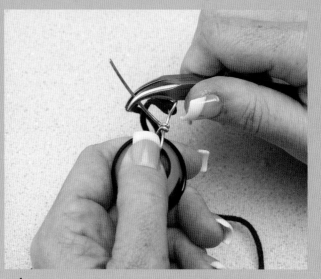

4 **Wire wrapping (optional)**
For a more secure attachment, or for connecting heavy items with wire, create a wire wrap. Form a loop and attach the embellishment as outlined in Steps 1–3, but instead of cutting off the wire, wrap it

GILDING

While rhinestones and wire definitely make your shoes glisten, gilding's the way to go for overall shine and brilliance. Working with metal leaf—whether it's fake gold or genuine silver—requires a delicate touch because the sheets are fantastically thin and can literally tear if you breathe on them too hard. But what an effect gilding has once you're done with the process! You can age it, or add a patina using stains specifically designed for that purpose, or leave it shining like a mirror. Either way, your new shoe design is sure to be the talk of any party.

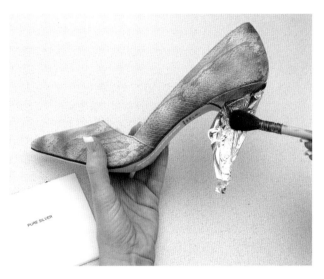

1 Adhere metal leaf
Use adhesive sizing to coat the area to be gilded. Allow the adhesive sizing to dry until it's tacky to the touch. Lay silver or gold leaf over this area and brush the leaf with a soft brush so that it sticks to the sizing.

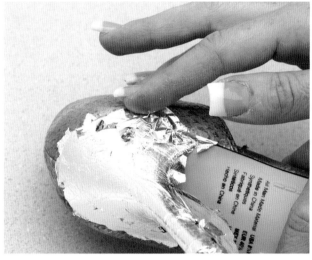

2 Cover area completely
As leaf is very delicate, it may tear while you adhere it. Fill in any holes or tears with small pieces of leaf.

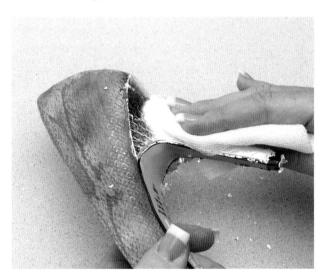

3 Burnish metal leaf
Lightly burnish the leaf-covered area of the shoe with cheesecloth to seal the leaf more securely and make it gleam.

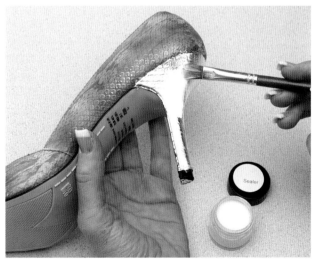

4 Seal gilded area
Seal the entire gilded area with a sealant designed to protect gilding. Allow the sealant to dry. Using sealant will give the gilding a longer life but may dull its appearance slightly.

sealing

Once you finish redesigning your fabulous new footwear, you will want it to last, won't you? Sealing the shoes helps them remain clean and often makes them water resistant. It also keeps paint from chipping, and it can prevent tears and snags in any fabric you've used. There is also a cosmetic reason for adding a sealant: It gives your shoes a polished look, both literally and figuratively speaking. A glossy finish will make them shine. Just make sure you let your shoes dry after applying the sealant according to the manufacturer's instructions.

1 Seal surface
To waterproof and protect your shoes and also to secure any items you've attached, seal the surface with an adhesive that remains flexible when dry. (I frequently use Mod Podge.) Allow the adhesive to dry completely before you wear the shoes.

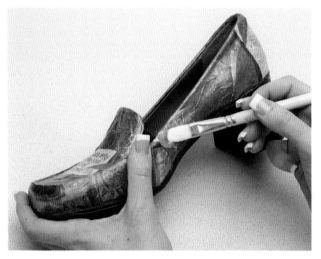

2 Add decorative elements (optional)
Mix glitter, mica or even paint into the adhesive as you seal the shoe to add a bit more decoration.

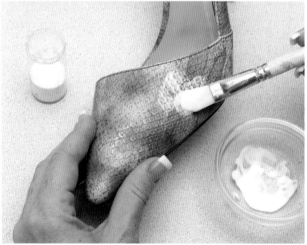

3 Highlight focal points (optional)
To highlight certain parts of your shoes, use a glossy adhesive on focal points and a matte adhesive for sealing the rest.

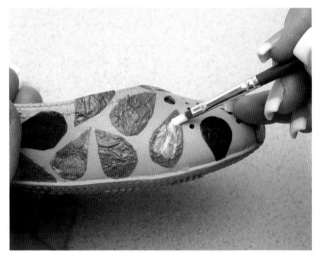

Save your shoes! Just because one shoe has a scuff on the heel or a slightly torn seam doesn't mean the pair belongs in the trash bin—especially after the shoes are finally broken in and perfectly sculpted to your feet. There's no need to curse anymore after stumbling off a curb and scraping the side of your favorite pumps. You just need to know a few tricks for disguising the little bumps and boo-boos that occur as a result of normal wear and tear. There are plenty of ways to mask small problems and also to camouflage bigger blemishes. Sometimes you'll even improve on the shoe's original design by adding some beautiful ribbon or a strategically placed rhinestone or two. Why buy a new pair of shoes when it'll just take a few minutes to transform the ones you've loved so much?

 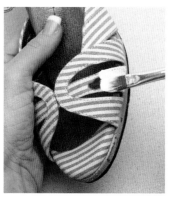 

STAINS

Whether you've spilled coffee on your espadrilles or your two-year-old has taken a pen to them, there's an easy remedy for the ensuing stain. Paint is a good choice, as is decoupage with paper or fabric. If you opt for paint, you may need to use a few coats on the area to truly obscure the stain. In that case, make certain your shoes are fully dry before stepping out the door in them. Paper and fabric are also great camouflage, but be careful when working with patterns—particularly if that pattern is on your shoes. Make sure the materials you choose complement one another.

SCUFFS

Fabric serves as a great cover-up for scuffs and scrapes. Ribbon works well too: It can finish off fabric edges or work on its own, particularly if the scuff mark's not too wide. When working with a shoe that's a single color, try using a patterned ribbon or fabric that incorporates the same hue. If you're thinking that this involves different techniques than the ones you've already read about, think again! To apply any of these fixes, just use the same methods you'd use if doing a redesign on an undamaged shoe.

 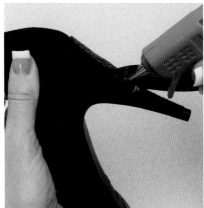 

open seams

If a seam is torn wide open across the length of the shoe, your first stop should be the shoe repair shop. But, if it's a small tear—under 2" (5cm)—you can seal the rip closed yourself using a hot glue gun. After that, adding trim or ribbon all around the edges of the shoes works well and fashionably to mask the injury. No one will know there was once a nasty tear lurking beneath the ribbon.

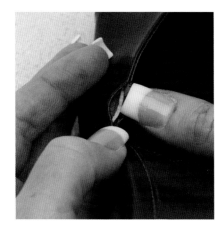 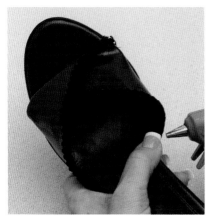

Viva Las Vegas Stilettos

Once, as I drove toward Las Vegas and the casinos began to rise up from the desert sand in the distance, it seemed to me that the famous Strip resembled an enormous glittering confection, a candy-coated cake that Dalí might have created. Any design inspired by Vegas must have radiant contours—the bigger and more angled the better. Stilettos alone just aren't enough, but gild them with genuine silver like this pair and you'll be ready for the high rollers' table. The rhinestones not only match Vegas's flickering lights; they also have the sugary feel of red licorice and gumdrops. And the *Q*s on your toes will let everyone know you're the queen of any room you enter.

material list

- A pair of stilettos
- Pearlescent paint
- Thin trim or ribbon
- Rhinestones
- Glitter
- Silver leaf
- Deck of cards
- Hot glue gun and glue sticks
- Adhesive sizing
- Sealant for metal leaf
- Water
- Small dish
- Paintbrushes
- Scissors
- Tweezers or needle-nose pliers

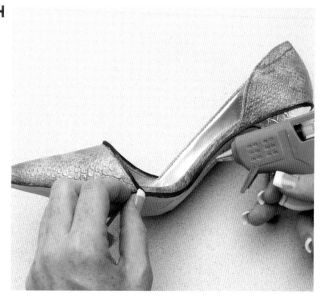

To start, mix the paint and glitter in a small dish, and then thin the mixture with water to make a sparkling color wash. Paint the shoes with a thin layer of the color wash, and then set them aside to dry (see *Painting*, page 23).

Now it's time to gild the heels and any other part of the shoe you want to draw attention to. I gilded the outside of my shoes as well as the heels—the better to catch the light when strolling into a party. Follow the directions for *Gilding* on page 34. Real silver leaf can discolor as it oxidizes. If you like that look, then let it oxidize! If you don't, use a sealant to prevent this. Allow the sealant to dry completely before continuing to work.

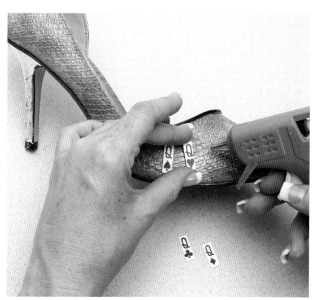

Heat up the hot glue gun and apply a short line of glue along one of the edges you'll be adding trim or ribbon to. Carefully place the trim on top of the glue and press the trim into place. Repeat this process until you've finished encircling your shoes with trim (see *Adding Trim*, page 28).

Select the 4 queens from the deck of cards and then cut out the Q and suit emblem from both corners of each card. Adhere the Qs to the front of the shoes with hot glue so that they form a row following the side contour of the shoe.

Glue rhinestones above and below the Qs to highlight them (see *Embellishing with Rhinestones and Beads*, page 29). To protect the tips of your fingers from burns, use tweezers or needle-nose pliers to handle the rhinestones. Next, add a line of glittering rhinestones along the side of each shoe. Alternate the rhinestones' colors to add some extra dazzle.

Finally, seal the shoe and embellishments, if you like (see *Sealing*, page 35).

Tips, Tricks & Crazy Things to Try

Although it's easy to get impatient while you're waiting for the adhesive sizing to dry, make sure the entire area you'll be gilding is tacky, not wet, before attaching the metallic leaf. Otherwise, you'll end up with a gooey mess rather than a sleek accent.

Head over Heels: Shoes with Heart & Sole

CAROLYN DEVINNY

I want to be Carolyn DeVinny when I grow up. She heads The DeVinny Group and is a commute consultant, which means she helps companies reduce their pollution contribution. "We work with employers," she explains, "to get their employees to their jobs in some way other than driving alone." Most people don't realize that once companies reach a certain size, they're required to have ride-sharing programs and such in place, at least in the state of California. (You may think we're nutty out here, but we were at the forefront of the environmental movement long before it became fashionable.)

Carolyn's been doing this for twenty years, and her client list has been nothing short of stellar: DreamWorks, General Electric, Cedars-Sinai Medical Center, Intuit, Whole Foods Market, Yahoo!, Abercrombie & Fitch, Barnes & Noble, and even the Los Angeles Lakers have benefited from her expertise. All in all, her company has contributed to over a thousand plans covering a half million employees. On top of that, she has worked with the U.S. Environmental Protection Agency and is a trustee for the California State Parks Foundation.

Now, how many of us can say that what we're doing is clearly and unequivocally benefiting the world? If I were Carolyn, I'd sleep very well at night, dreaming of translucent skies and untainted breezes. But given her gusto and creative mind, it wouldn't surprise me if all that brain activity of hers keeps her up sometimes. Even when it comes to her shoes, her feelings run deep and are crystal clear. She refers to her absolute favorite pair, bar none, as her "bright red hooker heels."

"They were for my young, hot and single journeys," Carolyn states of those sky-high shoes. "When I was heading out on a hot date, those were the shoes I wore." She says this like that's all in the past. She may no longer be single but, believe me, she's still hot and youthful. She got married just five years ago. And for those dum-dums who claim women over forty don't have a chance at marriage, especially if they're successful, I dare them to say that to Carolyn—who's far more dazzling and passionate in her midsixties than any twenty-year-old cover girl. Even melanoma couldn't bring her down. The woman's too full of life, and she doesn't linger at the halfway point with anything she does.

But back to those hooker heels. They had a very pointed toe and were about as high as standing on tiptoe. Nevertheless, Carolyn says, "They were very comfortable." Comfortable stilettos—is that possible? "I wore spiked heels with pointed toes so much," she explains, "that my foot had kind of cramped together. My feet and forward motion were accustomed to it." Those flaming red shoes were so memorable that Carolyn can recall exactly where she got them—in Oakland, California, in the Kaiser Center at Joseph Magnum's, which has long since closed.

That's not a big surprise, considering she bought those beauties forty years ago and wore them for fifteen years. That would put her in northern California in the late 1960s and early 1970s, and they didn't call it the "Summer of Love" for nothing. With those shoes, there must've been a lot of hot dates. She did, after all, wear them so much that she had to have them reheeled every six months. "They didn't make heels strong enough back then," she claims. "They'd disintegrate." I'm not so sure that's the whole story, though.

When I ask if she still has these shoes, she tells me she's searched all her closets but couldn't find a trace of them. Apparently her sister had helped her pare things down a year or so ago and those red-hot heels must have been a casualty of that. Carolyn says, "I wrote a nasty note to my sister, 'You made me get rid of my hooker heels!'"

At least the memory of them remains. Personally, I think it's time she bought another pair. You can, after all, wear bright red and be very green at the same time—especially if you're Carolyn.

Rhinestone Rider Boots

There may be a few people somewhere who wear cowboy boots merely for practical purposes: people who run ranches, for example, who really do wind up on horseback most of the day. Other than that, it seems to me that those who wear cowboy boots want people to notice them—and their boots—in a very big way. So why be shy, especially when you have so much room to play with? Emphasis is the key when it comes to altering cowboy boots. Highlight their height, the bootstraps, and the feet that stomp to country music. Give all those stitching details new life by making them sparkle and dance. So what if you've never sat on a horse? Announce to the crowd that there's a feisty filly in the mix when you stride in wearing these.

material LIST

- A pair of cowboy boots
- Metallic paint
- Metallic trim or ribbon
- Beaded trim
- Freshwater pearl strands
- Round rhinestones
- Oval rhinestones
- Hot glue gun and glue sticks
- Fine-tipped paintbrush
- Scissors
- Tweezers or needle-nose pliers

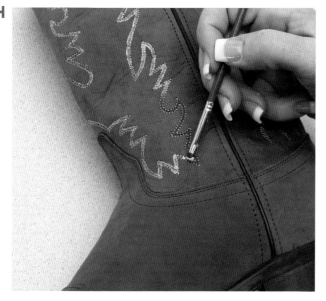

Paint the stitching on the boots with metallic paint and a fine paintbrush (see *Painting*, page 23). This will really call attention to all that stitching, which so often seems to just blend into the boot. Be careful not to smudge the paint when you turn your boots over to start painting the other side. Remember to paint the stitching on the front and top of the foot.

Use a hot glue gun to apply a vertical line of glue down the side of the boot, and press a strand of freshwater pearls into the glue (see *Adding Trim*, page 28). Repeat on the other side of the boot. Glue a piece of metallic trim or ribbon on both sides of each strand of pearls to complete a gleaming band down the boot's leg. Use the hot glue gun to add trim along the top edges of the boot, too.

To draw attention to the lower part of your boots, encircle the ankle seam with beaded trim. Glue beaded trim along the foot of the boot where the upper meets the sole as well. If you'd like, you can also add the same trim along the sides of each bootstrap. If you add trim to the bootstraps, you'll need to be careful when you're getting into and out of your boots or you might accidentally yank the trim off.

Now for the real sparkle: Use your tweezers or needle-nose pliers along with your hot glue gun to affix 2 bands of oval rhinestones across the top of the foot (see *Embellishing with Rhinestones and Beads*, page 29). Next, add oval rhinestones all around the boot where the leg meets the foot, right beneath the beaded trim. I left a small space between the rhinestones here, but that doesn't mean you have to. For more flash, make yours a solid band of rhinestones without any breaks.

Finally, dot the sides of the boot legs with round rhinestones placed in a way that will accentuate the boot's stitching. You've already highlighted the stitching with paint; now you can accentuate certain curves or points in the stitching by gluing rhinestones next to them. You can even glue rhinestones on top of the painted stitching if you'd like.

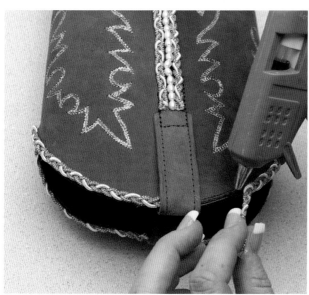

Tips, Tricks & Crazy Things to Try

If you think pearls are too expensive to consign to your boots, visit your nearest bead store for a pleasant surprise. Freshwater pearls cost a small fraction of what traditional pearls do—and they'll make your boots truly unique.

Head over Heels: Shoes with Heart & Sole

JENNY DOH

Whenever I enter Jenny Doh's office, I feel like the least creative person on the planet—or the least creative person that Jenny knows, at any rate. She's the editor in chief of *Somerset Studio, Belle Armoire* and twenty-nine sister publications, as well as director of publishing at Stampington & Company. As a result, Jenny's office overflows with unique and wonderful things, ranging from mixed-media collages to elaborately beaded apparel and all arts in between.

Jenny and Stampington have been generous to me. But even though my jewelry's been on the cover of *Belle Armoire* and my shoe designs have appeared in *Belle Armoire*'s *Altered Couture*, I always feel undeserving when I stand amid all the genius in Jenny's office. She sees some of the finest work from around the world and works with Stampington's capable staff to create magazines that are as memorable as they are beautifully produced.

Each time I've met up with Jenny, she's brilliantly put together. Her style is sophisticated but unpretentious, colorful but not overpowering, so I was understandably curious about what her favorite footwear would be. I thought she might choose something I hadn't seen before, something that was cutting edge, and perhaps even complicated. She prefaces her decision by saying, "In all honesty, I'd say that my favorite pair is my next pair," but then settles in to tell me her story, which is a delight in terms of both the elegant simplicity of the shoes' design and the serendipitous way she found them.

"I'd been wanting a pair of cowboy boots for so long," she tells me. "I knew I'd have to pay a pretty penny for them," especially for ones suited to her discriminating taste. But her discerning eye picked out exactly what she was looking for amid the castoffs at a local yard sale. "I saw them from afar and thought how wonderful they looked," she says. "I couldn't believe they were my size." These milk-chocolate brown boots "were broken in and distressed to perfection," she says. That buying them only plucked ten dollars from her pocket makes those boots even more of a treasure.

"I took them into my car and put them on right then and there," she says. "They're totally marvelous. I feel like a prairie princess in them." Where does she wear her boots? "To work. To shop. To play," she says, "and just to putter around the house." They're the perfect complement for all the facets of her life, whether she's chasing down her kids; out for a stroll with her husband, Gerardo; or deciding which distinctive designs to include in the pages of a magazine.

From the way she describes the boots' effect on her, it's clear that Jenny must have loved playing dress-up as a child—and probably still does. "They make me feel super feminine and at the same time super strong, like a super sassy and chic cowgirl," she tells me. In the same way an actor uses a costume to express a character she's about to portray, Jenny turns to her footwear to inspire her for the day ahead. "I often start composing my outfit with the shoes," she says. She spends much of her day searching for unexpected designs to delight a reader's eye, but she also has an enormous staff to supervise. "If I have to conduct some serious business meetings," she continues, "I wear my patent leather pointed toes—and you know what? They get me in the mindset and help me get focused for the task at hand: serious business."

Given her appreciation of the feelings that an unfussy pair of boots can evoke, she's the perfect person for her position, though how she keeps all those magazines straight is beyond my comprehension. "In many ways, I think shoes help me prepare for the different roles I have to play… as a mom, a career professional, wife or goofy friend." She then adds, "We frequently hear that a person can wear many hats. Well, I think it's not hats, really. It's shoes."

Paper Mosaic Flats

Say the word *mosaic* and most people imagine something elegant and colorful. Say "Let's make a mosaic design," and their faces fall as they imagine something that is difficult and messy and involves too many tools. I say, "Hah!" to that, especially with this design, which isn't complicated at all. Mosaics don't have to be! Simply put, a mosaic is a decorative design created by using colored pieces of material. It doesn't have to end up looking like a face or a landscape; it isn't required to have any pattern at all. What's consistent is the idea that the pieces coalesce in some way that's pleasing to the creator's eye. That's not complicated or messy. In the case of this design, no tools except a paintbrush and scissors are involved.

material LIST

- A pair of flats
- Suede-look spray paint
- Decorative papers
- Matte-finish white craft glue
- Glossy-finish white craft glue
- Cardstock
- Drop cloth
- Newspaper
- Paintbrush
- Scissors

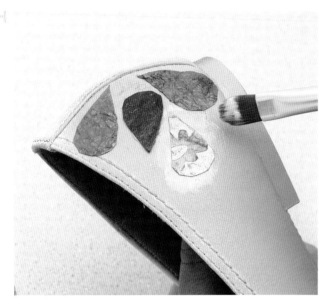

Spread out a drop cloth in a well-ventilated area. Set the flats down on top of the drop cloth and stuff their insides with some crumpled newspaper to keep paint out of the inside of the shoes. Spray-paint the shoes following the manufacturer's instructions (see *Painting*, page 23). Let the first coat of paint dry, then add a second coat and let the shoes dry thoroughly.

While the shoes are drying, you'll have plenty of time to make the paper pieces for your mosaic. To make your pieces fairly consistent, first draw on a piece of cardstock the form you've selected and cut it out. Use this template to trace the shape onto sheets of decorative paper. Cut out at least 75 pieces to start. Save that template, though, because you may need more pieces before you're finished.

Before gluing anything onto your shoes, assemble the paper pieces on a tabletop and begin creating your mosaic pattern, making sure the pieces appear to interlock like a mosaic. Try different arrangements until you're completely satisfied with your pattern. Then brush white craft glue onto the back of each paper piece and press the pieces onto the shoes, following the design you've already laid out (see *Decoupaging with Paper*, page 25).

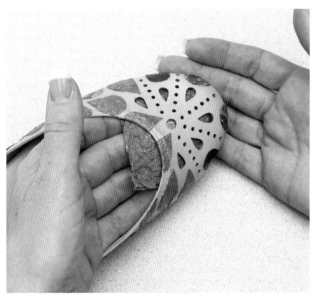

If your shoes have decorative cutouts in the front, as mine did, snip from one of your decorative papers a piece that's large enough to cover the entire cutout area. Brush white craft glue onto the top of the paper and insert it, glue side up, inside the shoe, beneath the cutouts. Press the paper into place beneath the holes until it is securely in place. By placing the paper underneath, you make the design show through the cutouts. Once the glue dries, trim away any excess paper.

Cover the entire shoe with a thin layer of matte-finish white craft glue to seal the spray paint and the paper pieces (see *Sealing*, page 35). Allow the glue to dry, then brush glossy white craft glue onto each paper mosaic piece. This will add shine to the design and highlight the texture of the decorative paper pieces, which will show off their pattern that much more.

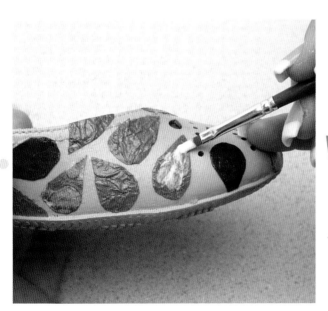

Tips, Tricks & Crazy Things to Try

I usually wear latex gloves when I use spray paint. Try it—gloves keep all that paint from sticking to the backs of your hands and creeping under your nails.

Head over Heels: Shoes with Heart & Sole

norma snyder

One Saturday morning a few years ago, I sat outside Norma Snyder's office, awaiting her ministrations. The office door opened, and she walked out with a client whose face was smooth and clean. "It looks great," she said as she examined her grateful client's skin. Once I was in her office, Norma showed me a photo of someone whose face was horribly swollen and pitted with acne. "That's not her," Norma said, referring to the client who'd just left, "but that is what her skin used to look like." I recalled the even-toned visage I'd just seen and marveled.

Skin is Norma's vocation, and to say she uses her skills to change people's lives for the better is no exaggeration. Most facialists in Los Angeles cater strictly to vanity, working to make surgically pulled faces look like they haven't been. While Norma has a celebrity clientele (given her knowledge, skill and location that's to be expected), the clients she loves to boast about are those, like the one I'd briefly met, whose lives have been transformed by her: teenagers who are no longer the butt of cruel high school humor and professionals who now feel confident that their clients listen to their words rather than stare and make unfounded judgments based on their appearance.

But I'm making things sound very sober where Norma's concerned. In fact, she has a wicked sense of humor, and the two of us have some running gags we'll keep to ourselves. It's no wonder that when I ask her about her favorite footwear, I hear "my little hug bunnies" in her reply. "Years ago I had a pair of big pink fuzzy slippers with a bunny face and ears," she tells me. "I'd slip my little feet into them, and they were my little hug bunnies. I wouldn't wear them anywhere else except in the house, but they made me feel all warm and secure."

Norma is a blue-eyed blonde and a lean tennis player, so these are not the shoes one would think she'd name as her favorites—unless one knows her as I do. "I've got a few pair of Manolo Blahniks in the closet that I love," she says with her delicious British accent. She then quickly adds, "but so does everybody," and continues talking about her "hug bunnies."

She bought them in Europe more than ten years ago, and they lasted for years because they were made from sheepskin. "They were something like Phyllis Diller would wear at her most outrageous," she says, "but they had a certain sentimental feeling, and they were wonderful." Those bunny slippers outlasted one marriage and carried on almost to the next one.

In addition to her "hug bunnies," Norma had another pair of shoes she felt sentimental toward for an entirely different reason. "I had one beautiful, drop-dead gorgeous pair of sandals that I never got to wear because of foot surgery!" she says wistfully. "They were champagne colored, four inches high, and cost a fortune." Norma had two toes broken due to bunions, and she had to have a couple of toes reset because they'd become crooked and were forming corns between the toes. She suffered through serious surgery and a long recovery. "My feet feel all better," she says, "but I can't wear heels anymore, so I never got to wear those shoes. I finally gave them away a few years ago." With typical humor and humility she adds, "That should be the worst of my problems."

Norma, by the way, is the best advertisement for her own work. Since I've known her, and we think that's at least twenty years, she's always appeared at least fifteen years younger than she actually is. Given that she works in Los Angeles, I'll keep that number to myself, but, suffice it to say that if your skin is in her hands—or as Norma and I jokingly say, if she's the one popping your pimples—you're in the best hands there are and your life could very well be better for her kind care.

Goth at Heart Heels

Is there anyone who hasn't gone through a Goth phase? Black clothes, black eyeliner, black jewelry—it's all so wonderfully macabre and irresistible, isn't it? I preferred red lipstick to black myself, but everyone has their own take on it. Even if you're past that phase—or at least pretend to be when you're at the office—that doesn't mean you can't hearken back to it now and then. Why not let your shoes show off your darker, more dangerous side? We all have a spare pair of black heels somewhere in our collection. Granted, the jeweled spiders and skull beads might be a little harder to come by, unless it's Halloween time. But almost every town has at least one store that specializes in ghoulish things—after all, someone needs to cater to the next group obsessed with black attire and all things Goth.

MATERIAL LIST

- A pair of open-toed high heels
- Oxidized silver chain
- 2 skull beads
- 2 spider charms
- Hot glue gun and glue sticks
- Wire cutters

Fire up your hot glue gun, and get ready to attach chain trim along the top edges of your shoes (see *Adding Trim*, page 28). Work a short segment at a time to keep the glue from drying before the chain is attached. Spread a line of glue, then press the chain into the glue carefully so that the hot glue doesn't seep through the holes in the chain and singe your fingertips. Also, keep the chain slightly away from the very edge of the shoe, or it may irritate your skin when you wear the shoes. Crisscross the chain across the front of each shoe to create a spot for your ghoulish focal point.

With the hot glue gun, attach a skull bead to the toe of each shoe where the chains cross (see *Embellishing with Rhinestones and Beads*, page 29). Use the spiders to make macabre hats for the skulls. If you can't find the perfect spider charm, try using spider earrings, as I did. (They were the only decent looking spidery things I could find.) Use wire cutters to clip off the ear wire from the back of each earring. That way, you'll have a flat surface to work with. Glue the spider directly on top of the skull as it's facing you, and you will have a truly spine-tingling new shoe design. These shoes would also be stunning in red—blood red!

Tips, Tricks & Crazy Things to Try

Skulls—real or otherwise—are usually round in back, so you'll have to be careful gluing them into position. Make sure they lie as flat as possible and that you use enough hot glue to hold them firmly in place. Use the chain to help support the skulls if needed.

Head over Heels: Shoes with Heart & Sole

CATHLEEN ALEXANDER

If you're ever about to get deported from Mexico, the land where they celebrate the Day of the Dead, you should have Cathleen "Cat" Alexander with you. No, it wasn't drugs that got me into trouble, at least not the illegal kind. Cat is now an independent film producer with the films *Young, Single & Angry* and *Park Day* under her belt, and I, of course, am doing this. But back in the mid-1990s we managed to get into a pile of trouble doing humanitarian work in the Mexican state of Chiapas following the Zapatista rebellion.

The same attributes that make Cat an excellent producer are what make her the best friend to have when you've just been nabbed at a checkpoint heading into rebel territory carrying letters and antibiotics. (Like I said, the drugs weren't illegal.) Given that Cat's such a big risk taker it's amazing how steady she remains in tense circumstances. She never makes a situation a bigger drama than it already is, she just digs in to get things done, which in this case included getting us to the airport before Mexican immigration could formally boot me from the country.

The one place Cat plays it practical is her wardrobe. "I'm definitely a very safe shoe person," she says. "I like to find shoes I can wear with almost everything, usually black or brown and very versatile. And I almost never wear high heels." Given that she's been blessed with height as well as flaxen hair and radiant blue eyes, she already stands out in a room no matter what.

But a few years ago, a pair of three-inch heels drew her in and wouldn't let her walk away without them. "It was a whim," she says of buying the dark green leather sandals with burnished gold accents. "I saw them, loved them, had to try them on." The fact that they were on sale made them even more irresistible. "It was one of the few times I've actually dared to spoil myself," she adds. That's because when she's not in indigenous Mexican villages helping to build schools, she's pitching in to help anyone else who needs it, whether it's a friend who's moving or the crews doing cleanup in South Central Los Angeles following the riots in 1992.

Cat's three-inch heels accompanied her to the Cinequest Film Festival, for the screening of *Young, Single & Angry*. She also took the heels to the Cannes Film Festival, but they stayed in her suitcase because the parking situation there was so bad that her feet became her primary form of transport. "These shoes are not made for walking," she explains, "though if I wear them all night at a party, I don't have to soak my feet the next morning."

Contrary to what everyone imagines, the filmmaker's life is anything but glamorous. However, for those events and occasions when she can set her producer's togs or jungle boots aside for something more alluring, these favorite heels are the shoes her feet tiptoe toward. "I feel like I'm playing dress-up when I put them on," Cat says. "It's the one time I center my outfit around my shoes. They're dressy, but they're not formal, and I'm tall in them—very tall!"

We both caravanned with the Zapatistas from Chiapas to Mexico City when they went there to address the Mexican Congress. As they addressed the huge crowd in Mexico City's *zocalo*, we watched from our hotel room along with Blanche Pietrich, a reporter we knew from *La Jornada*. In her article the next day, Blanche referred to our little group as *guaposas*. The translation's tricky, but it's sort of the equivalent of "glamazon"—a tall, confident and beautiful woman. Cat knows how to scale everyday dramas down to their proper size, and the way she handles them makes her an invaluable friend, whether it's on a Hollywood film set or at an army checkpoint. *Guaposa*—no word describes Cat more aptly, especially when she's got her heels on.

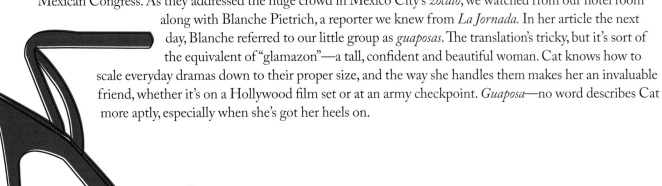

Crazy Quilt Granny Boots

Hanging on the wall in my sister Emily's living room is a large quilt my great-grandmother Adele Stevens made. Adele is close to my heart because she raised my mother during Mom's early years. I also refurbished Adele's old sewing machine, foot treadle and all. Now, you're probably envisioning a rustic quilt composed of squares, but Adele made a crazy quilt using leftover sewing scraps. She, like most of the women of her generation and before, made all the clothes for her family, and she did it all at the sewing machine I refurbished. That quilt hanging on my sister's wall looks a little like these boots, though without the frayed edges and the photo. People ask me how I come up with my more unusual designs. Just look at the size of the hat Adele's wearing—that's her picture on my boots—and you'll know exactly which genes my crazy ideas come from.

material LIST

- A pair of granny boots
- Metallic paint
- Assorted fabric scraps
- Lace scraps to match the fabric scraps
- Assorted ribbons and trim to match the fabric scraps
- Photo
- White cotton fabric
- Hot glue gun and glue sticks
- Rubber cement or fabric glue
- Liquid seam sealant (optional)
- Iron-on transfer paper
- Iron
- Newspaper
- Water
- Small dish
- Paintbrush
- Scissors

Before you begin working, remove the laces from your boots so they don't get covered with glue. Stuff the boots with crumpled newspaper so they hold their shape as you glue the fabric onto them. You probably don't want to finish your boots only to find you can't get your foot inside them!

Collect scraps of fabric, and choose 3 or 4 coordinating fabrics to use on your boots. Cut the fabric into different shapes and sizes, then begin arranging the pieces on a tabletop or draping them on the boot to see how you want to place them. If you want the fabric pieces to have neat edges, apply a liquid seam sealant or glue to the edges to hold the threads in place. If you'd like your fabric to be a bit frayed, run the fabric between your thumbnail and index finger to set some of the threads free.

Brush rubber cement or fabric glue onto the boot, then let it sit for 15–30 seconds so that the adhesive won't soak through the scraps. Position the fabric carefully and press from the center outward to secure it in place (see *Decoupaging with Fabric*, page 27). Use the same technique to add a second piece of cloth, and then another, and another—you get the idea. When attaching fabric to your boots, I suggest working from the toe backward or from the heel forward, and working in the same direction on both boots. You're more likely to wind up with boots that match this way. Unless, of course, you like asymmetry, in which case, work any way you like!

Layer pieces of lace over the top of some of the fabric to enhance the romance of your design. Trim the lace and fabric around all of the boots' edges to fit, particularly along the sole and around the shoelace holes.

Once you've added all the fabric you've chosen, use the hot glue gun to attach ribbon or trim around the boot where the upper meets the sole (see *Adding Trim*, page 28). This will cover up the rough edges of the fabric pieces. Use a different ribbon or trim to cover the other edges of the boots. Trim along

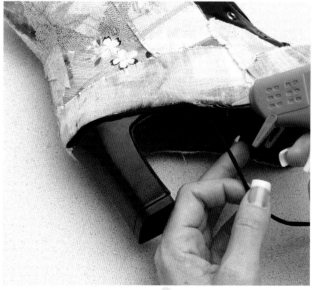

the top edge, the shoelace holes and any other area you'd like to accent.

Search your photo albums for a wonderful old photo of a family ancestor, then scan the photo to create a digital image. Create an iron-on transfer using the image (see *Using Iron-On Transfers*, page 31). Affix the transferred image to the outer panel of your boot using a hot glue gun, rubber cement or fabric glue—whichever you're more comfortable using.

Frame the transferred images with trim or ribbon. If you'd like, add another color to your frame using a different trim. Using 2 colors together will emphasize the photo even more.

For a final touch, embellish the bootlaces. Pour a bit of metallic paint into a small dish and mix it together with water to make a color wash. Dip your fingers into the wash and run your bootlaces through your fingers to add a bit of color. Set the bootlaces aside until they've dried completely, then lace the boots. Remove the newspaper from the boots, put them on, tie them and take a stroll around the neighborhood.

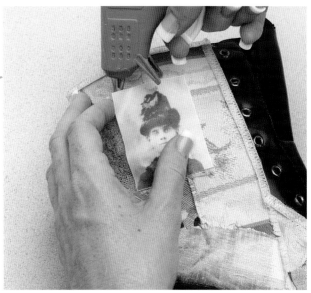

Tips, Tricks & Crazy Things to Try

Before gluing the fabric pieces onto your boots, try tapping them to your boots so you can see what your design will look like before you do anything permanent.

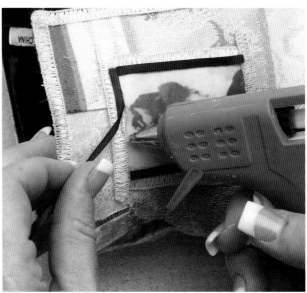

Head over Heels: Shoes with Heart & Sole

karen soucy

Sometimes the best thing a writer can do is just get out of the way. I know that Karen Soucy has a spirit as generous and expansive as the summer sky because of all the help she's given me and my company in her role as the associate publisher and advertising director of *E: The Environmental Magazine*. That she has a young son was news to me but no surprise, given her warm, maternal nature. But the story behind her favorite shoes is an unexpected wonder, and the best way to convey it is to use the words Karen spoke to me on the phone one afternoon:

"I'm going on thirteen years at *E* magazine and it feels like two and a half. When I think of where the environmental movement was twelve years ago and how now it's just booming all over the world, it's so exciting. As clichéd as it sounds, I have to say what I do is so much more than a job. It's a way of living, and I'm grateful to be in a position where so much information comes my way. I feel like I'm laying the groundwork for companies to prosper and to keep meeting challenge after challenge. And to get paid for all that is just amazing.

"My favorite shoes were a pair that belonged to my mother. I grew into them around the year she passed away and out of all the things of hers that we saved, I really gravitated toward those shoes. They were a rust-colored pair of open-toed sandals with a strap around the ankle. I remember they had a thick faux-wicker heel and were your quintessential 1970s wedge. I think if anyone ever saw them today they'd go, 'Eeeuuw!' but they were just right for the 1970s.

"When Mom passed away in 1978, she was forty-eight years old. I was fourteen. I lost her way too young. I went to a Catholic high school, and Mom died between my freshman and sophomore years. Her shoes met the school's dress code, so they literally became part of my uniform. I wore them to school every day and almost everywhere I went.

"Originally, she had breast cancer. They found it too late, and the treatments she was given back then weren't very good. It metastasized into various forms and eventually lodged in her spine. For those last two years, she couldn't walk at all, so she couldn't wear those sandals anymore. After she passed away, wearing them was really my one connection to her left in the physical world. I was literally walking in her shoes. They reminded me of how much I missed that mother-daughter connection, of things that I would never be able to share with her, of things that I lost out on because she died so young. I remember I wore them until they literally fell apart. The stitching just gave out and there was no salvaging them.

"During my teen years, Mom was so proud that I was doing things she never had the chance to do—even just going to high school, because she wasn't allowed to. Her family immigrated here from Italy in the 1920s. She was born in the 1930s and grew up during the Great Depression and then the war. It was a very large, old-school Italian family. All the men in her family got to go to high school and on to college if they wanted to, but all the girls in the family had to stay home and work. Of all the things my Mom lived to see, my going to high school was special for her because she never got that opportunity. I was given permission to flourish without any limitations. I think that was one of her greatest gifts to me.

"Whether you're five or fifty-five, when you're a daughter and your mother dies the impact is everlasting. It's been thirty years since she died, and sometimes I'm still that fourteen-year-old girl trying to deal with things."

Ribbon Stripe Pumps

I always love strolling down the ribbon aisle at a craft or fabric store. I just want to gather all the strands together and play amid the colors. Even though I don't sew, I can never resist getting a ribbon or two in the hopes that I'll come up with something to do with them. I find beautiful brocade ribbons especially hard to resist. When I do have a project that uses ribbon, I always seem to end up with yards and yards left after the project's done. If you also have a ribbon fetish, then this is the shoe design for you. At last all those vibrant leftovers can find a home. Unfortunately, now that I've designed the shoes, it takes even longer to drag me from the ribbon aisle.

material list

- A pair of open-toed pumps
- Ribbons (lots of them, including at least 1 that's 1" (3cm) wide or wider)
- Thin trim or ribbon to match the shoes' soles
- Hot glue gun and glue sticks
- Scissors

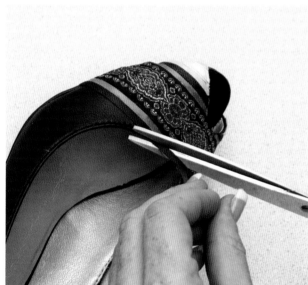

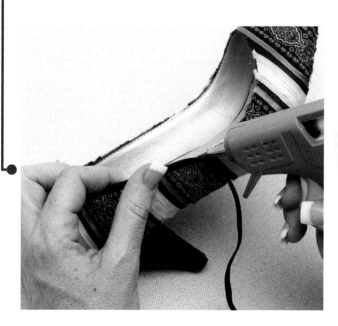

Before you do any gluing, lay out the ribbons on a tabletop and determine what design you want to make with them. I chose 4 single-colored ribbons that match the colors of the thick brocade ribbon I'd picked as the focal point of my design, and I decided to alternate the ribbons. Though I chose 4 colors, you should choose as many or as few as you like. Don't just think vertically; the ribbons can be arranged horizontally, as well.

Once you decide how you want to arrange the ribbons, heat up your hot glue gun and affix the first ribbon at the front tip of the shoe (see *Adding Trim*, page 28). Use very sharp scissors to clip the ribbon to fit on both sides. Continue to attach ribbons 1 by 1 in the order you've chosen, and slowly make your way toward the back of the shoe, snipping as you go. Make sure to have several glue sticks on hand for this project because you'll have a lot of ribbon to glue.

Chances are, once you've reached the back of the shoe, things won't line up exactly the way you thought they would, but don't worry! Instead, cut a piece from the thickest ribbon or whichever ribbon is the focal point of your design. The piece should be long enough to cover the back seam of the shoe between the top of the heel and the top of the shoe. Line it up carefully and glue it into place to draw both sides of your ribbon pattern together.

To tidy up all those uneven ribbon edges, cover them with thin trim or ribbon in a color that matches the soles of the shoes. Glue the trim along any openings in the shoe, as well as where the sole meets the upper.

Tips, Tricks & Crazy Things to Try

Before gluing each piece of ribbon in place, stop and make sure you're following your pattern correctly. It's very easy to accidentally leave a color out—take it from someone who knows all too well.

You can switch the order of the ribbons for a more varied look, but still be sure you have a plan before you start gluing and stick with it. Why? Because you might want some sort of color consistency or pattern, and that's tough to accomplish on the fly.

Head over Heels: Shoes with Heart & Sole

joan boorstein

Longevity in Hollywood, both in front of and behind the camera, is not the norm. Consistently working on projects you truly care about? That's even less likely. As Senior Vice President of Original Programming at Showtime Networks, Joan Boorstein has managed to do the unthinkable. She's been at Showtime for years and has shepherded shows like *This American Life, Brotherhood* and *The United States of Tara* from script to television screen and managed to get daring movies like *Soldier's Girl* and *Rated X* made, a trick even for premium-channel cable programming.

With her quick smile and temperate voice, Joan has an ease with the producers, writers and other talent who work on the projects she oversees. As someone who's responsible for acquiring potential shows and movies for Showtime, she's also known for having superb taste in material and for knowing what will work for the network. The latter is no easy task. Amid the mountains of scripts and story pitches she encounters are many that are compelling and even well told. But once the other necessary considerations—like budgets, ancillary markets and Hollywood's personality politics— are accounted for there remain very few projects that can thread that particular needle. The reason for Joan's standing in her industry is that she understands how to coordinate and weave together all these intricacies the way a designer works a color palette.

What makes Joan so interesting to talk to when it comes to her shoes is that, though she moves through a high-profile milieu, she has some very pedestrian health issues to consider. "I have to be careful with the shoes I get, because I have totally flat feet and sciatica," she says. Comfort has to be her first concern, especially when she's standing around on a film set all day.

This, however, butts up against another issue common to so many: At five feet, three inches in height, she thinks she's short. Mind you, she could stand barefoot next to some very famous leading men and still look them squarely in the eye. Nevertheless, she insists, "I can't stand the feeling of being short. I never wear total flats."

So, what does Joan wear to the Emmy Awards? A favorite pair of sling backs, with a bow and slight platform in front and a high heel in back. "They have enough padding in front for a nice feeling of balance with the height of the heel," she says. "They give me equilibrium and don't make me lean forward."

From what's televised, it looks like everyone at the Emmy Awards spends the entire time sitting. But in reality there's a lot of standing before, during and after the ceremony. That's when a lot of old-fashioned networking gets done. Fortunately, her favorite pair of heels make the situation tolerable. "They aren't tight when I'm standing in them," she says. "They're not pressing into the ball of my foot or throwing my back off. They fit my foot just right."

The same practicality Joan applies to shoe shopping has helped keep her career grounded as well. Some people in entertainment get lucky and have a hit or two. Joan's successful run has been built honestly. She's smart, she cares, she works hard—and everyone knows it. I mentioned the considerations that go into acquiring a project. But that's like getting to Everest's base camp—there's still the rest of the mountain to climb. Once Joan has found a script that can pass through the needle, she then has to marshal the right people to work on it. This usually involves working with personalities that are always unique, often eccentric and sometimes tyrannical. Next, she supervises the project through production and guides it through editing and sound design until finally (often after years of work) it's broadcast for all to see. I have to believe that is Joan's greatest reward, though I'm sure when there's an award show or two to attend as a result of all that endless work, she's thrilled to get those heels out.

Shining Star Struts

Failure is surely the most reviled *F* word in the American vernacular, yet I believe I've learned more from my failures than I have from my successes. I'd spent months putting together a book of wire jewelry designs only to have the publisher go belly-up. I was tempted to banish the book's projects to a dark corner of my garage. Instead, I searched for other outlets and one of those jewelry pieces wound up on a magazine cover. Another necklace from that would-be book included stars made from silver wire. When I was walking along the Hollywood Walk of Fame on Hollywood Boulevard, strolling over all the stars planted in the sidewalk, I had the idea to transfer the stars from that necklace to this shoe design. The lesson? When something goes awry, even if it's just a design that doesn't work, keep your eyes open and make yourself expect another opportunity. It's sure to arrive eventually.

material list

- A pair of high-heeled sandals
- Silver chain
- 18- or 20-gauge silver wire
- Silver jump rings
- Hot glue gun and glue sticks
- Wire cutters
- Flat-nose pliers
- Round-nose pliers

Use a hot glue gun to apply a line of glue along the edge of the shoe and carefully press the silver chain into it (see *Adding Trim*, page 28). Keep adding glue and chain until you've covered the edges of the shoe. Cross the chain over itself near the toe. Use wire cutters to clip the chain once you've finished this step.

Now it's time to get starry eyed! To follow my design, make 6 wire stars for each shoe—5 for the front and 1 to hang from the heel—a total of 12 wire stars. To begin work on the first star, cut a 5" (13cm) piece of 18- or 20-gauge silver wire with the wire cutters. You will create the star's points by bending the wire around the flat edge of a pair of flat-nose pliers. Start by bending the wire out at a slight angle. Move the pliers to the other side of that bend, then bend the wire outward at a 45-degree angle. Press the wire against the side of the pliers firmly to make the angle as sharp as possible.

Regrip the wire with the pliers on the other side of this new bend. Bend the wire again, this time inward at a 45-degree angle. Continue making these bends in the wire, alternating between outward and inward angles, to form the 5 points of the star. As you bend the wire, you'll be able to see the star forming. Keep the image of a 5-point star in mind as you work, and let that image guide your hands as you work the wire into its proper shape.

Once you've made all 5 points, create a loop at the end of the wire by wrapping it around the round-nose pliers (see *Making Wire Embellishments*, page 33). Wrap the other wire end 2–3 times beneath the loop to form a wire wrap. Trim any excess wire, if necessary, with the wire cutters. Repeat to make a total of 12 stars or whatever number you want for your design.

Next, decide how to space the stars along the chain attached to the shoes. Do you want to place the stars all together in the center, or do you want to space them evenly apart? Run a jump ring through the top loop of each star and fasten the stars along the chain according to your design plan.

Finally, don't forget to flip your shoes around and hook a star onto the back of each one to make sure no one ignores your heels.

Tips, Tricks & Crazy Things to Try

Practice really helps when you're new to working with wire. You should count on making a few lopsided stars before you wind up with one you like, so be sure you have plenty of extra wire.

Head over Heels: Shoes with Heart & Sole

LISA ELIA

I think launching a new business these days is akin to what early explorers experienced when they set out in search of new lands. The skies before you look clear enough as you take your first steps or sail your first few miles. But who knows what awaits you beyond what you can see. Will there be fair weather or storms? Will you encounter kindly folk or wind up battered and bloody? Or, worst of all, will you wind up off course and lose your way altogether?

Thus far, my journey with my Rebagz™ handbags has been fruitful, and much of that is because Lisa Elia has been my compass. The home page of the Web site for her company, Lisa Elia Public Relations, bears the heading "Creating Integrity," and that happens with everything Lisa does. She goes far beyond what a publicist normally does, which is getting the media to write articles and such about a client, something she's been wildly successful with, especially on my company's behalf.

In many ways Lisa has been my mentor. Her spot-on suggestions and business advice have helped me make much better business decisions, and she's been a soothing voice when yet another shipment has been held up or when sales suddenly far outstripped our capacity at the time. When she gets us another great article, it seems she's even happier than I am. No matter the topic, I always end a conversation with Lisa wiser and more enlightened than when we began it.

An important component of Lisa's work is knowing when to be discreet. As an example, I can't tell you exactly where she's worn her favorite shoes. Suffice it to say they've sauntered through some of the swankiest events in Hollywood, particularly those linked to certain awards given in the entertainment industry, because some of her clients host the parties.

The first time Lisa was invited to one of these events she knew she had to find something special. Enter a pair of tall sandals with thin silver straps that wrap around the ankle. "I'd been looking and looking," says Lisa, "and I just loved them the minute I saw them." They have lots of clear, shiny crystals clustered all along the front of the foot, and though they're very chic, they're also quite comfortable. "They're sparkly, and I love silver," says Lisa. "I can have the plainest thing on and the shoes will make the outfit. But I can also wear them with something ornate and not feel like they're over the top." They'll be around for a long time, both because their look is timeless and because she doesn't get to wear them very often. "How often do you get to dress up like that?" she asks.

Even more important for exceptional occasions like these is that, according to Lisa, "These shoes make me feel confident and very put together. I always get loads of compliments."

As I mentioned before, every conversation with Lisa brings more insights. Why should our shoe discussion be any different? "Shoes really change how you present yourself to the world," she says. "Think of the term *well-heeled* and what it means. In a lot of cultures, people are often judged based on the shoes they're wearing."

That brings my thoughts back to undiscovered lands and embarking on new terrain, commercial or otherwise. When Lisa raves about my handbags and my business, she gives me all the credit. That's just her charitable nature. But I truly could not have made this trek without her and her expertise in all areas, not just publicity. Even if by some miracle I could have scrambled up this mountain without her help, it would have been a much lonelier climb.

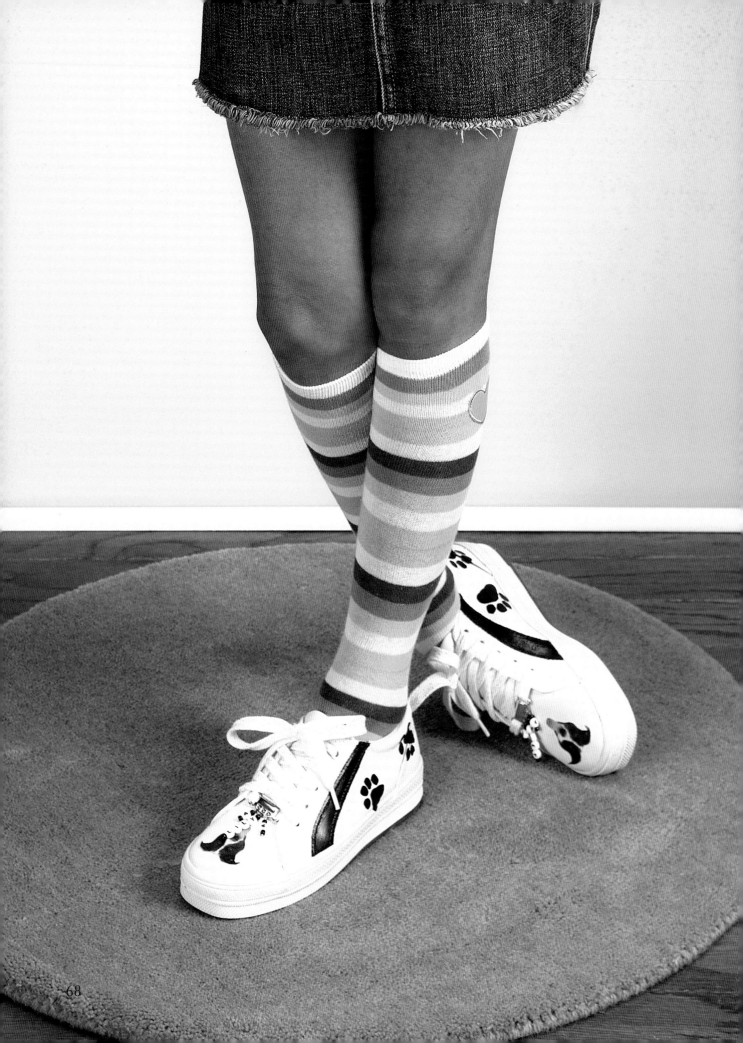

Rocket Lily Sneakers

That's my girl! Lily was two years old when I took the picture that appears on these shoes. We'd been playing fetch at the dog park, and nothing, not even a bowl of sloppy wet dog food, makes her happier than chasing after a tennis ball. The farther it's thrown, the better. Since Lily's a rescue, it's anyone's guess what breeds lurk within her wiry body, but there's got to be a thoroughbred speedster in there somewhere. One of the reasons I picked Lily out of the litter was because she had the same markings as Cookie, my dog from my childhood. I wanted this book to include a design that would be easy to do with kids, and those thoughts of Cookie and this photo of Lily provided the inspiration. Tossing the family pet into the mix makes it more fun for everybody.

material LIST

- A pair of sneakers
- Fabric paint
- Photo
- White cotton fabric
- Alphabet beads
- Round beads
- 6 1½" (4cm) head pins
- 2 multihole brackets
- Paw-print rubber stamp
- Hot glue gun and glue sticks
- White craft glue (optional)
- Iron-on transfer paper
- Iron
- Small paintbrush
- Needle-nose pliers

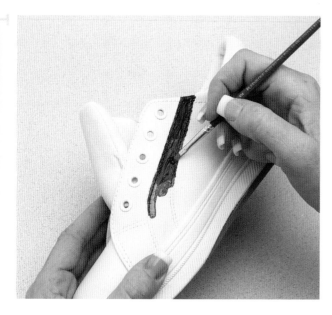

Use the fabric paint and paintbrush to fill in or create racing stripes down the sides of the sneakers. Allow the paint to dry completely. Instead of ink, use fabric paint with the rubber stamp to create the paw prints on the sneakers. Chances are, the paw prints won't turn out perfectly, so keep your paintbrush standing by to fill in any gaps as necessary. You can also paint the paw prints freehand instead of using a stamp, if you prefer.

Find a photo of your pet's sweet, adorable face and create an iron-on transfer with it (see *Using Iron-On Transfers*, page 31). Attach a fabric photo to the front of each sneaker with a hot glue gun. Coat the top of the photo with a layer of white craft glue to help seal and protect the photo.

Next, use alphabet beads to spell out your pet's name, your child's name or your very own moniker. String these beads onto a head pin, and use pliers to create a small loop at the end of the head pin (see *Making Wire Embellishments*, page 33). String other decorative beads onto 2 other headpins and make loops in the end.

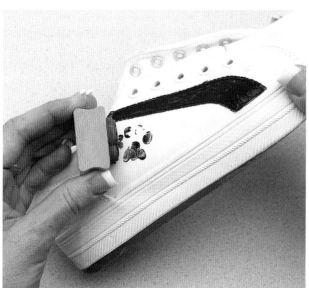

To attach these beaded pins to the sneakers use a multihole bracket. Slide a bracket to the center of each shoelace and slip the loops at the end of the head pins through the holes of the brackets.

Once you're done, lace up your sneaks and go fetch!

Tips, Tricks & Crazy Things to Try

Make sure you give the fabric paint plenty of time to dry. Always follow the manufacturer's directions for drying and setting the paints, and you're sure to have great results.

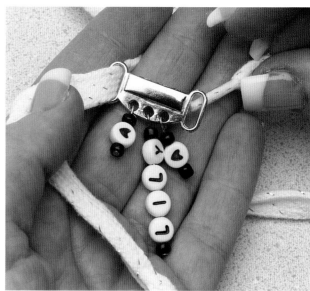

Head over Heels: Shoes with Heart & Sole

DEBBIE ROESTENBERG

Cinderella's glass slippers may have helped transform her from scullery maid to princess, but imagine the blisters she must have had once the party was over. There are far better journeys, and far more comfortable shoes to wear while you're traveling.

Taking those journeys can be tricky these days, especially if you're going by plane. When your connecting flight's been cancelled and the ticket agent repeats messages like "all flights full" and "tomorrow afternoon at the earliest," you want Debbie Roestenberg's number. She has somehow snagged me a seat in the worst circumstances—partly because of her twenty-five-plus years of experience as a travel agent, but mostly because she cares too much to leave any client stranded.

That caring nature led her back to school, first to earn her associate of arts degree and then to continue on toward a degree in sociology at Chapman University in Orange, California. "I want to give back to society," Debbie says, "and I think I may want to do that by going into social work"—as if fielding desperate calls from stranded holiday travelers hasn't been challenging enough.

Among her requirements as a student were classes in "exercise science," which they called phys ed when I was in school. Debbie opted for an aerobics class. Since she hadn't been exercising she badly needed new sneakers, so off to the mall she went. There she found the gym-class equivalent of Cinderella's slippers: a pair of size nine sneakers in heather blue with white stripes. She really liked the color, and their bouncy feel made her think the chore of doing aerobics might be a bit less painful.

"The first time I took the class, I did it because I had to," says Debbie. "But the second and third times I took it were just for pleasure, because I liked how much healthier it made me feel." And she didn't stop there. She and her husband Casey, her prince for the last twenty-one years, like to take long walks around Irvine Regional Park and she wouldn't think of wearing anything other than her heather blue sneakers.

These sneakers haven't just stayed in California. "Did you ever see that movie *The Bucket List*?" Debbie says, referring to a movie about two men who are determined to live out their life goals before they die. "Getting into Chapman and going to China were on my list." In 2005, she took care of the latter with a two-week trip, and her favorite shoes went with her. Her heather blues walked her around Beijing, the Great Wall and Xi'an, where the famous Terracotta Warriors were unearthed and are now on display. "I even got to meet one of the farmers who discovered them," she says, as I try to keep my history-geek envy to myself.

These new experiences and her newfound physical strength have brought other benefits. "It's all given me more confidence," she says. The exercise also helps her handle the stress of, say, a statistics class that is as annoying as it is difficult.

Noting the years of wear and tear, Debbie finally decided it was time for a new pair of sneakers. She recently bought a second pair of the same kind, but favorites become favorites for a reason. "I keep going back to the old pair!" she exclaims. "There's just something special about them, even though they're more gray than blue now." When you consider how far those shoes have taken her, you know it's not just comfort that makes this pair of faded sneakers more exquisite than any glass slipper ever worn in a fairy tale.

Pumped-Up Polka Dot Stilettos

On a trip to Antarctica, I had the good fortune to be accompanied by many professors and specialists. One knew about whales, another knew about geology, and someone else had spent a great deal of time among the penguins. Our penguin guide wore a pair of high-top sneakers that were either incredibly bright yellow or outrageously purple. Sadly, I can't recall which. But I do remember telling him they were like exclamation points on his feet. Why do we like to wear something vivid on our feet? After all, normally people look at faces, not feet. Yet shoes, particularly unique ones, really do add punctuation to our appearance. Sometimes they're a quiet comma or period. But other times they beg a question—"Where did you get those?!"—and, occasionally, they truly astound. Clay embellishments are perfect for the latter because they add vivid hues and distinctive dimension to any design.

material LIST
- A pair of stilettos
- Acrylic paint
- White acrylic paint (optional)
- Decorative paper
- Polymer clay
- Hot glue gun and glue sticks
- Glossy-finish white craft glue
- Paintbrush
- Decorative craft punches
- Rolling pin
- Wax paper
- Razor blade

Separate ⅓ of the clay from each of the polymer clay bricks with the razor blade; store the rest of the clay for another project. Slide 1 clay chunk between 2 sheets of wax paper and roll the clay out with a rolling pin. Flatten the clay into an even sheet, approximately ¹⁄₁₆"–⅛" (2-3mm) thick, then do the same with the other clay colors.

Lay the flattened clay sheets on top of each other and roll them into a log. Roll the clay tightly to avoid any air pockets. Next, cut discs ¼"–½" (6mm–13mm) thick from the clay log and bake them according to the manufacturer's instructions.

While the clay is in the oven, paint the shoes (see *Painting*, page 23). If the paint color is substantially paler than the shoe, you may want to prime them first with a coat of white acrylic paint (see *Preparing Shoes for Altering*, page 22). Allow the paint to dry, and apply a second coat if necessary for full coverage. Add accents with another paint color, if desired. I painted the tips of my shoes' heels and the sides of the soles.

Use decorative craft punches to cut out several pieces from the decorative paper. Cut more than you think you'll need, just in case some of them tear. Before gluing the papers into place, lay them out on a tabletop or temporarily tape them in place on the shoes. Once you've decided where the shapes will go, attach them using white craft glue (see *Decoupaging with Paper*, page 25).

Once the clay pieces have cooled, determine how many to use and where to place them on the shoes. Make sure you decide the placement of the clay pieces before you break out the glue. Yanking them off after you've glued them in place can create holes in the paint and paper. Once you're ready, glue the colorful discs in place using a hot glue gun. Finally, brush a coat of glossy-finish white craft glue over the top of everything for extra shine and polish (see *Sealing*, page 35).

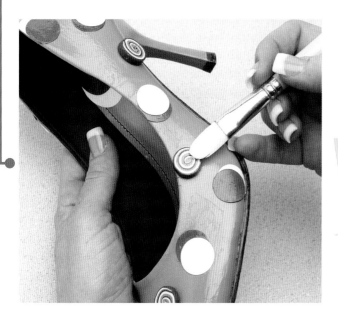

Tips, Tricks & Crazy Things to Try

Make more clay discs than you think you'll need for your shoe design. You can use any discs that remain to make jewelry to match your shoes.

Head over Heels: Shoes with Heart & Sole

TUCHI IMPERIAL

I don't understand people who insist that miracles appear by command the instant they're asked for or as images in their morning cereal bowl. When my dog sits on my command—an admitted rarity—that communication between two species is miraculous to me. Want to create something out of thin air? Just start a conversation using any piece of wireless technology. Even more magical are those fateful meetings or phone calls that materialize at just the moment you need them.

In my case, I received an e-mail from someone I hadn't heard from in twenty years. "This is Ruth Imperial. Do you remember me?" the e-mail read. "I go by Tuchi now." I was so happy to hear from her I shouted out loud. Tuchi and I had been inseparable during our first year of graduate school. The hours and projects taxed us to within an inch of sanity, but having this engaging and dedicated Filipina as my ally made it manageable. The following year, though, Tuchi got pregnant, and understandably left school to raise her son.

Tuchi wrote that she'd discovered that my recycled handbag designs are manufactured in her native Philippines, where she'd returned to live with her family. She asked if I was coming there any time soon; if so, she wished I'd get in touch with her.

That she'd found me was astonishing. That she could do it from the Philippines via the Internet was miraculous.

I called her on the phone just as soon as the time difference would allow. "Tuchi!" I yelled into the phone. "I'll be in Manila a week from now!" She told me she was worried about having my handbags made there. "I have to protect you," she said. "You're in the land of the pirates!" She did, in fact, end up providing invaluable counsel about protecting my designs and business. She explained cultural nuances to me with the same clarity and generosity that had made her such a remarkable friend in the first place. It was like having a much beloved sister returned to me.

When I saw Tuchi for the first time in twenty years, she looked exactly the same. She's as glamorous and age defying as she is endearing. It's no wonder, then, that her favorite shoes are a pair of silver sandals with three-and-a-half-inch heels and thin straps covered with crystals. "It's a damn sexy shoe!" she says. "I bought them in New York knowing that I would wear them at my cousin Erika's wedding." Tuchi was one of the event's sponsors, so naturally, it was spectacular. "It was absolutely memorable because hers was the first family wedding we had in many years," she says. "The reception hall was decked out like a Far Eastern fairy tale, and everyone special in my life was there celebrating my favorite cousin's important day."

Fortunately for Tuchi, her dazzling high heels were merciful. "I was dancing on them till the end of the night! They're sooo comfortable." And now she dances in them every chance she can. "I always try to make an excuse to wear those shoes," she says. "They make me feel like I could dance all night—and I have! For something that looks so fragile and delicate, they've gone through some heavy wear, and yet, miraculously, they look not a day older than when I first wore them. They're my magic shoes."

Tuchi deserves to have more fanciful evenings like that. She's raised a wonderful young man, and she is also the president of Quicklend Financing Co., Inc., a Philippine company she founded when she moved back there in 1993. "Our clients are middle- and lower-income people, very simple salt-of-the-earth people who keep me grounded," she says. And that's what Tuchi does for me.

If you're still not convinced about the magical and mystical aspect of Tuchi's e-mail, consider this: On page 67 you can read about Lisa Elia's favorite pair of shoes, and I swear they're exactly the same pair of sandals made by the same well-known designer! In a world full of shoes and individual tastes, how magical is that?

Stamp Your Foot Loafers

In the aftermath of the terrorist attacks on September 11, 2001, some of my creative friends questioned the importance of their art in a world so full of hatred and violence. Someone pointed out that under virtually all dictatorships artistic expression is cruelly limited. So in some ways, art can be a form of rebellion against loathing and aggression—and the filth they heap upon us. I admit walking around wearing shoes that reveal what you think may seem to be a small thing, but in some places, you could be arrested for it. Don't be shy. Make a proud statement with every step.

material LIST

- A pair of loafers
- Metallic paint
- Cotton print fabric
- Decorative papers
- Rubber stamp of a word or phrase
- Rubber stamp with an image
- Ink pad
- White craft glue
- Water
- Small dish
- Paintbrush
- Scissors

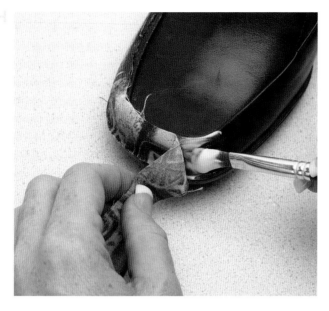

Cut a strip of fabric long enough to wrap around the front part of your footwear. Decoupage this strip of fabric onto the shoe (see *Decoupaging with Fabric*, page 27). If you have trouble fitting the cloth around the shoe, you can cut darts in the cloth to make it behave. Snip off any loose threads.

Next, cut strips from the decorative papers to cover both sides of the shoe. With this design, the more color the better, so don't be afraid to layer different colors. Decoupage decorative papers to the sides of the shoe, layering them and allowing the colors beneath to stick out a bit so that all of the colors are visible (see *Decoupaging with Paper*, page 25).

Cut a piece of decorative paper large enough to cover the top of the shoe. Decoupage it to the shoe, and then trim it as needed to fit.

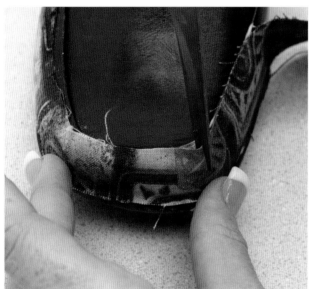

Cut out a rectangular piece of paper that will fit on the top of the shoe. I recommend paper that is a solid color, otherwise your stamped phrase or image could be difficult to see. Have extra paper standing by because it usually takes a few tries to get a great imprint (see *Stamping*, page 30). Check the stamp to make sure it's clean and dry so you get a tidy imprint. To add the color, either press the stamp firmly on the ink pad or rub the ink pad over the top of the stamp. Next, carefully place

Tips, Tricks & Crazy Things to Try

Although my directions call for both fabric and different kinds of paper, you can opt for just one or the other, if you'd like. All design decisions are entirely up to you!

the stamp on top of the paper rectangle and hold it steady. You can press down on the stamp firmly, give it a few solid taps—or both. Just make sure you don't knock the stamp askew or you'll wind up with an illegible mess. Put the stamped paper aside to give the ink time to set. Once it's dry, decoupage the stamped paper onto the front of the shoe.

Now it's time to use your image stamp. I chose a dragonfly because I liked the angles, as well as how graceful the figure was. Cut a rectangular piece of paper to wrap around the back of the shoe. Stamp the image on the paper, following the same process you used for the text stamp. After you've made the imprint and let it dry, decoupage it onto the back of the shoe, directly above the heel.

Once all of the glue has dried, mix some of the metallic paint with water in a small dish to create a color wash. Brush the color wash over the entire shoe to add a soft sheen to the design. Allow the color wash to dry.

Snip out several long, lean triangles from the decorative papers. Decoupage these as accents above and below the stamps on your shoes. You can glue just a single color into place or layer multiple colors—whatever suits your taste.

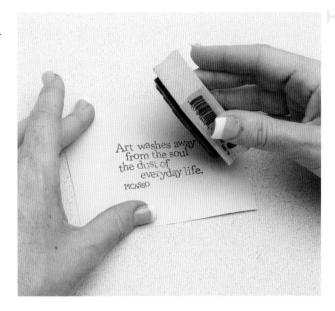

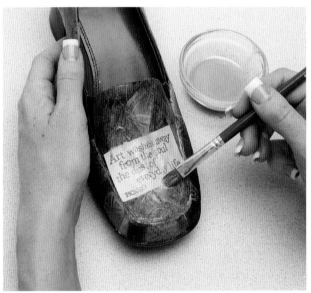

Tips, Tricks & Crazy Things to Try

I didn't add trim to this design because I liked the slightly ragged edges. If you'd like a neater appearance, by all means trim away.

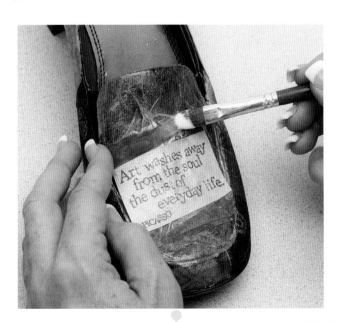

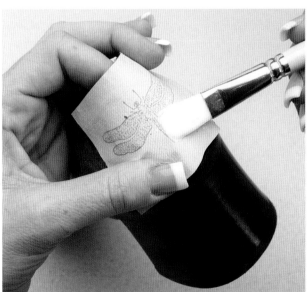

Head over Heels: Shoes with Heart & Sole

SHERIE POLLACK

I first met Sherie Pollack while trolling the corridors of UCLA's Melnitz Hall during graduate school, giddy from lack of sleep and desperate to find something to eat other than the offerings of Melnitz's ancient vending machines. In addition to finding better food, Sherie and I have seen each other through endless adventures, successes and upsets. No matter how many tears flow at first, the laughs always outnumber the snuffles. That Sherie can divine humor in the direst circumstances—including her own—is the thing I treasure most about her.

"Marty, it's Sherie," her message began, and in a tone I'd never heard from her. "I'm alright. I was in an accident. I just wanted you to know." Car accidents happen all the time in Los Angeles; it's the price of being car dependent in a crazy metropolis. But in Sherie's case, a speeding car had careened downhill into her lane and thoroughly, utterly crushed her car and body. Just consider her list of injuries:

· her sternum broken in two places

· every chest muscle torn

· her top left rib fractured in the front and back

· her right kneecap smashed by her car's cup holder—an injury that went misdiagnosed for two weeks

When I visited her at the hospital, breathing was difficult for her and laughing was painful, but she did both anyway. She was surrounded by mounds of gifts and was wearing the most adorable turquoise slippers someone had brought for her. She loved those slippers so much I thought they were the pair she'd name as her favorite. Instead, when asked about her most special pair of shoes, Sherie says, "It's just one shoe. I call it my accident shoe."

She was wearing her cherished leather clogs the night her life changed for good. These sepia-toned shoes had soles of wood, not plastic. "I'd had them for at least five years," she says, "and they were worn in and worn well. You could see the imprints of some of my toes through the top." One of them came off during the collision and lodged beneath the brake pedal. As the firefighters were cutting her out of the car, she asked one of them to please retrieve it for her. "My car was catching fire at that point," she says, "so he said, 'we'll get it later,' and pulled me out."

Within a few days, it became clear to Sherie that her life had now separated into two parts: life before the accident and life afterward. "That shoe and my underwear were the only things left over from my past life," she explains. "I wanted to go back and rescue the shoe left in the car, but by the time I was able to my insurance company had sold my car for parts." One shoe remains here with Sherie in her new life, while the other—her accident shoe—resides in the past, alongside her former existence.

She calls the clog left behind her accident shoe because she now realizes when you see a lone shoe on the side of the road, it's left behind from someone's car wreck. "That one shoe was always comfortable," she says. "It took me to and from good situations and bad boyfriends many times." She adds, "I'd also wanted to say good-bye to my car," as a way of acknowledging that that part of her life was over and, in its own way, complete. "But I'm so lucky," she says. "It could've been so much worse."

It's been nearly a year now since the crash, and Sherie's rehabilitation continues. Her body will never feel quite the same, but her mind and spirit remain as full of sunny vitality as ever, and she's always ready with tales of clueless hospital orderlies and about how her primary concern as they wheeled her into the emergency room was whether she'd worn the tattered or intact panties that day.

As I said, with Sherie there are always more giggles than snuffles.

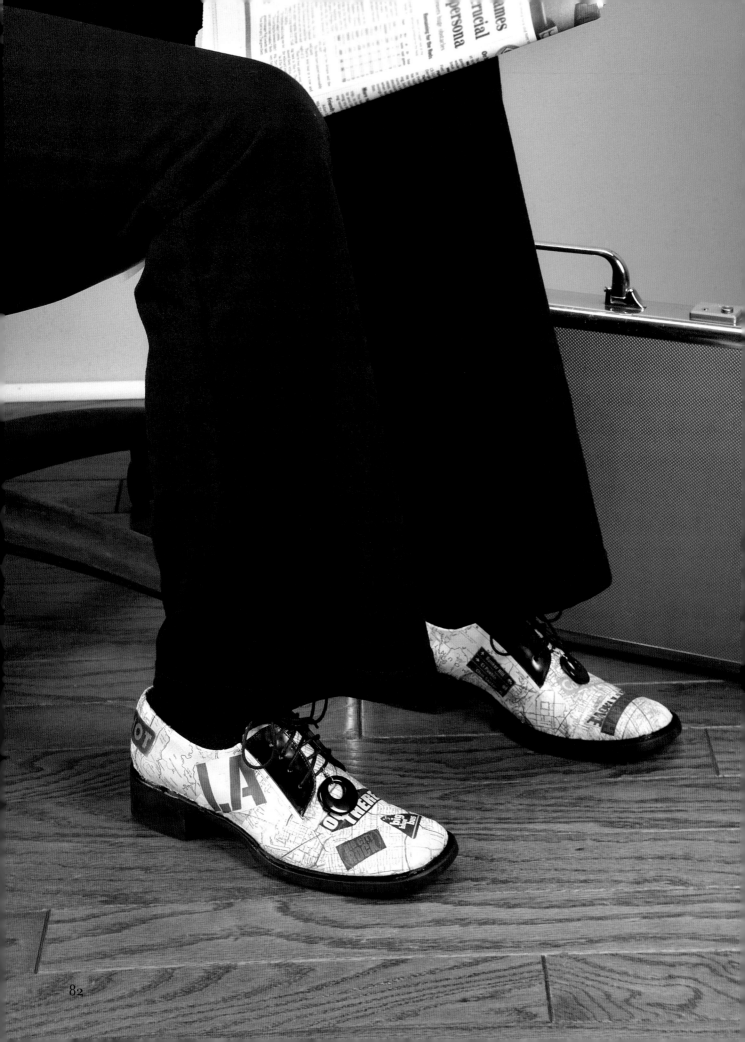

City Slicker Striders

The only way to truly know a city is to walk its streets. You can cover more ground by car, of course, but you also have to avoid distractions or you might end up locking bumpers with a patrol car ahead of you. When you're on foot, the whole point is to get distracted—by the boutiques, the landmarks and the feel of the sidewalk beneath your feet. Make a stop at a neighborhood coffee shop and kick back with the local paper to see what's going on. Newspapers offer a reflection of the city they're written in, echoing its pace and style, as well as its vernacular. Before your next trip, find a comfortable pair of walking shoes. Take a newspaper, either from your home town or from a city you've visited, and make yourself shoes reserved for strolling city sidewalks. Just don't forget to pack them next time you leave town.

material list

- A pair of walking shoes
- Maps
- Logos, phrases and words cut from newspapers and magazines
- Thin trim or ribbon
- 18- or 20-gauge wire
- 2 charms
- Hot glue gun and glue sticks
- White craft glue
- Paintbrush
- Scissors
- Wire cutters
- Round-nose pliers
- Needle-nose pliers

Remove the laces from the shoes and set them aside. Lay out your maps and snip out the most interesting parts, keeping the size of the pieces to about 3"–5" (8cm–13cm). Decoupage the map pieces onto the shoe to completely cover it, except for the sole and lace tabs (see *Decoupaging with Paper*, page 25).

Strategically place logos, phrases and words on different parts of your footwear. You can use the same word in the same place on both shoes, or you can go the asymmetrical route, as I did. Handle the newspaper and magazine bits delicately because they tear oh so easily, especially when wet with glue. Once you have everything in place and are satisfied with your design, brush a coat of white craft glue over the top to seal everything in place (see *Sealing*, page 35).

Use the hot glue gun to apply a line of glue where the sole meets the shoe's upper, then press one end of the trim into the hot glue. Encircle the entire shoe with trim, then clip the loose end neatly before gluing it down (see *Adding Trim*, page 28).

Use the wire cutters to cut a 5"–7" (13cm–18cm) piece of wire. Form a loop in one end of the wire (see *Making Wire Embellishments*, page 33). Wire wrap the other end of the wire around a charm. Once the shoes are completely dry, lace them with a charm dangling at the bottom center of each shoelace.

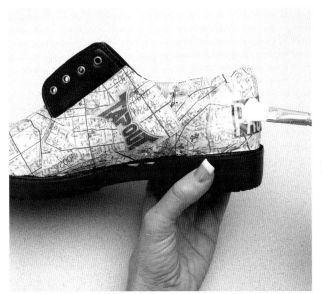

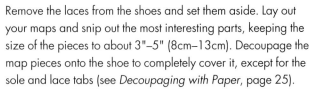

Tips, Tricks & Crazy Things to Try

Celebrate your hometown or a remarkable trip with these shoes by using local maps and newspapers. If you'd like to have shoes that match completely, you'll need at least 2 of each logo or phrase—which means you'll need to buy at least 2 copies of each newspaper or magazine you're clipping from so you'll have a matching set.

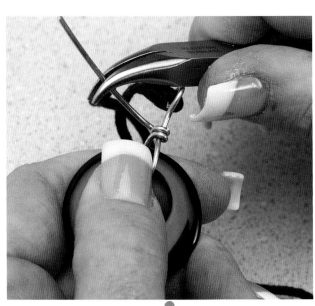

Head over Heels: Shoes with Heart & Sole

AUBREY MCCARY

I met Aubrey McCary when she was still Aubrey Williams. I'd gone to see the musical *Wicked* in Los Angeles and wound up sitting next to her. *Wicked* is a retelling of *The Wizard of Oz* from the so-called "wicked" witch's point of view and is a sympathetic tale about her and Glinda, the "good" witch of the story. There are battles between them, of course, but there are also moments of mutual reverence.

Aubrey and I chatted between acts and then again after the musical ended. She knew a great deal about theater and clearly had a poet's inclination. When she told me she was in the U.S. Army and would soon be heading to the Middle East, I admit I was flummoxed and worried. Though my concern remained unabated, I came to realize she's a poet warrior, a rare find these days, and stronger than any fictional woman we saw on stage that evening.

Aubrey represents the third generation in her family to serve in the U.S. armed forces, following in the boot steps of her father and grandfathers. As a child, she'd try to put her pint-size feet in her father's old army boots, to no avail. "I wasn't allowed to play with them because they weren't clean," she writes in an e-mail to me. "I was handed some toy 'princess' heels instead."

But Aubrey was drawn to those boots nevertheless and had her own pair of black leather combat boots at West Point by age eighteen. Unfortunately, these were recent army issue and not nearly so comfortable as her father's boots. "I spent hours trying to break them in," she writes, "even wearing them in the shower to mold them to my feet." She was plagued by ghastly blisters during training as she endured miles of road marches. And no matter how much she polished them, they never gleamed sufficiently to pass inspection, which just seems spiteful on the part of those boots.

As strongly as she was drawn to her father's cherished boots, she strove to get out of her own combat boots whenever she could. "I traded them for 'comfort shoes' like flip-flops and sneakers," she writes. "I indulged in shopping sprees for kitten heels and espadrilles." Contrary to what many people think, women warriors don't shed their femininity. "Despite working in such a predominantly male environment, I love shoes as much as any other woman," Aubrey writes. "I love ballet flats, stilettos, and skinny jeans tucked into knee-high boots."

Still, she had to wear her combat boots during those years at West Point, and as they adjusted to her feet she adjusted to them. The blisters eventually healed, and Aubrey began seeing where those boots would take her. She graduated in 2007 and shortly after I met her was deployed to Iraq and Kuwait, working in human resources and personnel. "It was a surreal experience," she writes. "I learned a lot in a short amount of time, and I helped send three thousand soldiers home to their families, which was an incredibly rewarding job."

So now those boots have come full circle, from being loathsome in Aubrey's eyes to being something treasured. "Shoes can say everything about who you are or who you want to be," she writes. "In those boots, I have marched endless miles, jumped out of airplanes, ridden camels in the desert, and even met the love of my life," which explains why she's Aubrey McCary now instead of Aubrey Williams. "I used to feel like my boots weighed me down. Instead, I realize they have carried me from adolescence to adulthood, from high school to domestic bliss, from my home in Indiana to the desert of the Middle East."

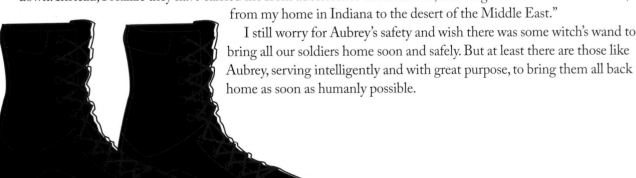

I still worry for Aubrey's safety and wish there was some witch's wand to bring all our soldiers home soon and safely. But at least there are those like Aubrey, serving intelligently and with great purpose, to bring them all back home as soon as humanly possible.

Over the Rainbow Slip-Ons

Some artists and designers know exactly what they're going to create before they begin because they see it vividly in their imaginations. My own mind's eye, however, could use a contact lens. When I design, I start with a vague idea that ends up requiring revision, sometimes a lot of it, in order for the project to work. I'd originally planned this shoe design for new moms and moms-to-be and to include amusing phrases like "Rub my feet, please," "This back needs a massage," and "I know what I'm expecting—how about you?" But once the colors were in place, I knew adding anything else would make the design too busy. I still think they're wonderful comfort shoes for expectant or worn-out mothers. They're just not what I originally envisioned. So don't get frustrated if what you initially plan doesn't satisfy you. Instead, keep working and let yourself be surprised by what unfolds before you.

MATERIAL LIST

- A pair of comfortable canvas slip-on shoes
- Broad-tip fabric markers
- Fine-tip fabric markers

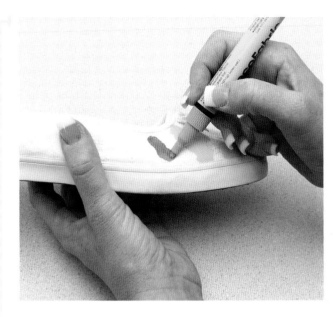

Before you begin working, decide in what order you want to use the different colors of your fabric markers. Even if you want your design to appear random, it's still a good idea to make some choices before laying marker to shoe so that you get an idea of how you'd like to space your hues. Set one of the brightest colors aside for creating accents in your design.

Next, start coloring! I stayed inside the lines (more or less), but you should feel free to deviate, depending on whether the shoes you've chosen have a pattern on them, as mine did, and whether you like that pattern. Alternate your colors, and work all the way around your shoe.

Take the marker you set aside for accents and begin adding embellishments. To help separate the colors on my shoes I filled in the small, floral patterns that were located in between the color sections.

Add other embellishments with a fine-tip fabric marker. I drew simple lines between the different color sections and also outlined the bow on the toe of the shoe. These embellishments will augment your accent color as well as bring out the different hues of your whole design. Set the shoes aside, and let them dry. Set the inks according to the manufacturer's instructions.

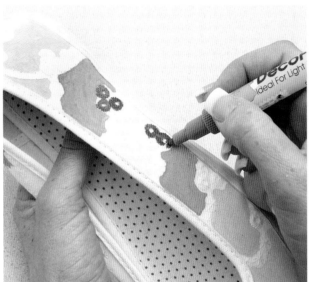

Tips, Tricks & Crazy Things to Try

You can also use fabric paints for this project. Just brush them on as you would any other paint, but follow the manufacturer's directions for drying and curing.

Head over Heels: Shoes with Heart & Sole

JENNIFER PERKINS

Leave it to Jennifer Perkins to have not one but four favorite pairs of shoes. Everyone else besides this crafty redhead (unless she's up and dyed her hair again) managed to narrow it down to one. But consider that right now, at this very moment, she has the following jobs:

· owner of Naughty Secretary Club (her online jewelry shop and blog)
· author of *The Naughty Secretary Club: The Working Girl's Guide to Handmade Jewelry*
· member of the Austin Craft Mafia (as in Austin, Texas)
· producer of the annual Stitch Fashion Show and Guerrilla Craft Bazaar
· editor of the Craft Artists Life blog at www.craftgossip.com
· teacher
· co-owner of a consulting company

You can surely understand why her footwear favorites are a tad multitudinous.

Oh, and Jennifer's also hosted *Craft Lab* and *Stylelicious* on the DIY Network—that's how I first met her. During *Craft Lab's* first season the producers somehow found me and put me on the show. After managing to set the record for saying the word *exactly* more times in a TV half hour than anyone ever had before, I broke that record the second time I was on. Jennifer, who could have been merely tolerant, was instead funny, teleprompter friendly, and a deft painter, glass etcher or anything else that was needed to make the show flow—or make her loquacious guest more comfortable. Like I said, the woman's a multitasker. Now, about her shoes…

"I wanted the most obnoxious pair of cowboy boots I could find," says Jennifer, "and I think I succeeded." Her boots have pink feet and pink tops and are black around the middle, with birds and flowers thrown in because there just wasn't enough going on already. As unusual and colorful as the woman who wears them, these boots are the most expensive twosome in Jennifer's footwear collection. I'm amazed she's managed to keep track, given that she stopped counting after acquiring two hundred pairs. "I'm on floor-to-ceiling shoe rack number three," she admits, "and into the fourth closet."

Jennifer loves how fresh-bought shoes make old clothes seem new again, and this is a woman who knows how to put a newfangled fashion spin on anything. It only takes one cyberstroll through Jennifer's jewelry store to realize she's addicted to accessories. She's dedicated two rooms in her house to her collection of jewelry, purses and—oh, yes—shoes. Another favorite pair of shoes are vintage and have "clowns, flowers and women from far-away lands all made of patchwork leather." Another one of her faves are a pair of pencil shoes—as in they look like pencils. The piece that wraps around the heel is the eraser, the shoe's sides are the yellow body and the toes look like pointy lead pencil tips. "It takes people a minute to get them," she says, "but once they do, the questions and comments just don't stop."

But wait! The shoes she wears most are the ones she got in London a few years back. "I spotted these men's tennis shoes with a purple toe, hot pink heel, orange stripes, aqua trim, green tongue, yellow trim and various rainbow dots along the rim of the rubber sole," she says, "and my heart melted." Fortunately, they had a small enough size for her or there might have been tears.

Yep, that's favorite number four. "What I love about shoes the most is that no matter how much I weigh my shoes always fit me," she explains. "I might not be able to get in the same blue jeans I could five years ago, but I have shoes from ten years back, and somehow that works just fine as a consolation prize." I don't know what the woman's thinking, because no one looks finer strutting down Austin's streets than Ms. Perkins in her pink and black cowboy boots.

Buttons and Bows Espadrilles

My late mother kept a tin of buttons in the chest of drawers she set aside for sewing. I'd love to be able to ask her now where they all came from, because there were so many and there was such variety. I've noticed that some craft suppliers now offer button collections, albeit much smaller than Mom's, and I think that's because there must be a lot of us who grew up with those tins of buttons. Mixing the buttons and ribbon bows together for this design reminded me of all the frilly dresses Mom used to put me in for holidays. I used pale blue and floral fabric because they reminded this T-shirt-and-jeans woman of those little-girl dresses from years ago. I don't miss how they itched, but I do miss the sight of Mom's proud eyes when I walked by her side wearing one of them.

material LIST
- A pair of espadrilles
- White acrylic paint (optional)
- Acrylic paint
- Fabric
- Ribbon
- Buttons
- Hot glue gun and glue sticks
- Rubber cement or fabric glue
- Tissue paper
- Paintbrush
- Scissors

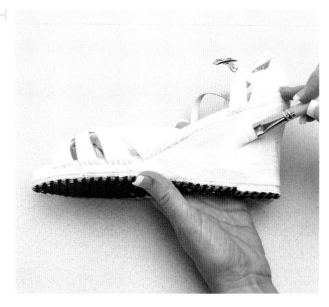

If you're using a paint color that's paler than the shoes you are working with, you may want to prime them first with a coat of white acrylic paint (see *Preparing Shoes for Altering*, page 22). Allow the white paint to dry, and apply a second coat if necessary for full coverage. Once the primer paint has dried, apply acrylic paint in a color of your choice (see *Painting*, page 23). It may take more than 1 coat of paint to make the color completely uniform.

After allowing the paint to dry completely, create a pattern for the part of the shoe you want to cover with fabric (see *Creating a Pattern*, page 24). Use this pattern to cut out pieces of fabric to cover the shoe. Brush rubber cement or fabric glue onto the shoe, and let it sit for 15–30 seconds or until it dries enough so that it won't soak through the fabric. Carefully press the fabric into the adhesive; start from the center and push outward (see *Decoupaging with Fabric*, page 27). Rub your fingers across the fabric to ensure it adheres as smoothly as possible without any air bubbles or creases.

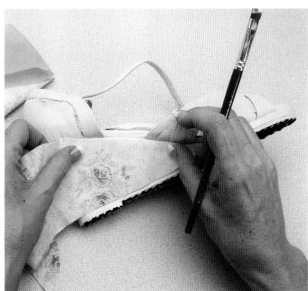

Fire up your hot glue gun, and add a line of glue along the sole of the shoe. Slowly and carefully attach ribbon all the way around the sole using hot glue (see *Adding Trim*, page 28). Run your finger along the top so that the ribbon lies flat against the shoe. Accentuate the heel by outlining it with ribbon, too.

Next, it's bow-making time. Clip a few 5"–7" (13cm–18cm) pieces of ribbon, and tie each piece into a bow. It takes some adjusting to make them flat and taut, so keep trying until they look the way you'd like.

With the hot glue gun, affix bows to each heel. You can also use bows to camouflage those untidy ends where the pieces of ribbon meet. Add colorful buttons at the top of the heel, just below the bow, and also on the front of the shoe. Pile buttons on top of each other, if you'd like, and add a bow or 2 on top for a touch of whimsy.

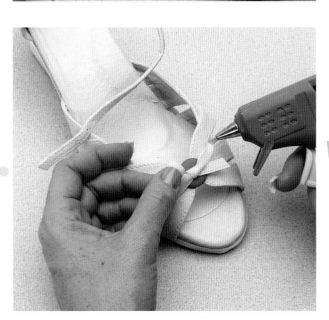

Tips, Tricks & Crazy Things to Try

If you choose fabric shoes, as I did here, make sure you have plenty of paint. Even after priming, canvas drinks up paint like dry earth soaks up water, so you'll need to do quite a bit of painting to get good coverage.

Head over Heels: Shoes with Heart & Sole

CHRISTINE CALLA

I date my company's beginning back to the first time I ever set out some of my handmade jewelry at a small street festival just to see what would happen. It was a blustery Saturday in April 2004, the last stormy day of that spring. Almost no one came, my teeth chattered all day, and it would have been an unmitigated disaster were it not for the new friend I found in the booth next to mine. As it turned out, Christine Calla was also taking part in her very first festival, and she, too, was selling next to nothing. But thanks to our proximity and the bond that shared duress often forms, a wonderful new friendship took root. That made up for everything, once my clothes were dry.

Christine's the customer service manager at a large apparel manufacturer, and she is the mother of three (she includes her husband in that tally). Like so many makers of handcrafted jewelry, she came to it as a form of therapy. Her husband was in a dreadful car accident several years ago, and she needed a way to soothe herself during his long recovery. After thoroughly cannibalizing her 1980s jewelry and giving away her creations as gifts, requests poured in from family and friends. So she thought perhaps she should get more serious about it, and that's how we came to meet on that gusty April day.

I don't recall what shoes Christine was wearing at the festival, but I guarantee they added inches to her height. There are few things Christine will curse about, but her size is definitely one of them. I tell her she's petite and lovely. She says she's just (choose your expletive) short. At least I can get her to agree with me when I say good things come in small packages.

It's no surprise, then, that her favorite shoes are a pair of chocolate brown suede platform wedges. "They're tall enough to give me some height," Christine says, "but not so high that I look like a rocker. They elongate my legs and they're graceful." It's also easier to keep her balance with a wedge than a stiletto. "You're not off kilter," she says. "I like how the wedge is even." She also loves that their peep toes and wraparound ankle straps give them a 1940s feel. "I like the vintage flair they have," Christine says, "and the ankle strap makes them sexy."

Versatility's vital to any working mother, and these shoes have proven to be very adaptable. "I've worn them to every kind of occasion, from conservative to funky affairs," she says. "I love that I can wear them for running around or dancing." And at work, they're just plain practical. "They work well when I have to transition from being the customer service manager to heading over to the warehouse to chase around after something." Because they're a neutral color, they don't clash with some of Christine's more unique outfits. "They work nicely with the funkier outfits I have," she tells me, "whether I'm wearing a Bermuda shirts or something trendy like a bubble hem."

With her sophisticated taste and generous heart, Christine has become a trusted advisor as well as a friend, and she has helped me steer my company in new directions—even to the Philippines, where she grew up and where I now have my handbags made. Her counsel has been invaluable, as have her design acumen and raucous sense of humor. We even coauthored a book about vintage jewelry designs, and she chuckles when she says she'll never do that again.

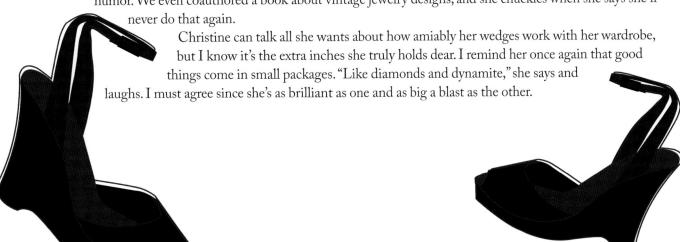

Christine can talk all she wants about how amiably her wedges work with her wardrobe, but I know it's the extra inches she truly holds dear. I remind her once again that good things come in small packages. "Like diamonds and dynamite," she says and laughs. I must agree since she's as brilliant as one and as big a blast as the other.

Flower Power Pumps

Bead shops are dangerous places. All those gleaming trinkets in countless colors and shapes call to me the way Romeo called to Juliet. Because of this, I have drawers full of teardrops, rounds, barrels and discs, as well as containers loaded with crystal, natural-stone and ceramic beads. Seeing as one can only have so many necklaces (and that one's friends have only one birthday per year), I've had to find other projects where I can use all those beads. Given that shoes and things that sparkle go well together, it was just a matter of time before some of those beads found their way out of the drawer and onto my footwear. It only took a hot glue gun to make it work. Fortunately, I've finally found a way to keep my bead addiction in check—I lock my wallet inside the car before venturing inside a shop.

material LIST

- A pair of pumps
- Teardrop beads
- Round beads
- Hot glue gun and glue sticks
- Tweezers or needle-nose pliers

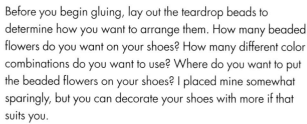

Before you begin gluing, lay out the teardrop beads to determine how you want to arrange them. How many beaded flowers do you want on your shoes? How many different color combinations do you want to use? Where do you want to put the beaded flowers on your shoes? I placed mine somewhat sparingly, but you can decorate your shoes with more if that suits you.

Once you've made your design decisions, plug in your hot glue gun and apply a small dab of glue onto the shoe. Press your first teardrop "petal" bead into place (see *Embellishing with Rhinestones and Beads*, page 29). Next, glue teardrop beads on either side of the first bead. Continue placing beads on either side of the first bead to create a circle of beads. Next, plant a globule of glue directly in the middle of the bead circle and roll a round bead into it to help secure your flower.

Decorate the shoe with as many flowers as you'd like. Then, glue just 3 teardrop beads on the end of the shoe, directly over the toe, and anchor them in place with a round bead glued at their tips. Do the same in the back, right at the top of the heel.

Tips, Tricks & Crazy Things to Try

You may want to practice gluing beads onto a spare piece of fabric so you can figure out how to space your petals. This way you can experiment to see what size you want your beaded flowers to be.

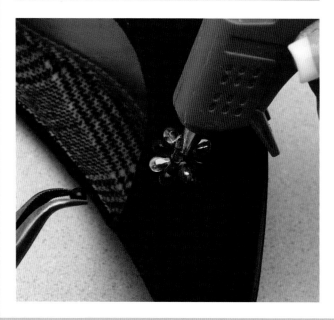

Head over Heels: Shoes with Heart & Sole

ELIZABETH TRACTENBERG

Anyone who thinks accounting is a dull and colorless profession needs to meet Elizabeth Tractenberg. For years she's guided me through the annual forest of numbers comprising my tax return, and she has shepherded me from employee to sole proprietorship to a limited liability corporation. I still don't quite understand all of the intricacies of all the different corporate entities, but she does, particularly as far as the tax implications go. More than that, she sees the art in numbers—and I don't mean in an illicit, sure-to-get-you-audited kind of way.

She creates symmetry in a balance sheet by making sure things are in their proper place. "Sometimes I'm up late at night working on a company's return," she says, "and I think, 'I can't believe I get paid to do this!'" She can instantly see when something's out of proportion and knows exactly how to restore order to an errant profit and loss statement. More than anything else, she loves to see the people and companies she works with thrive.

Elizabeth is also one of life's great enthusiasts, embracing all things in it, numerical and otherwise. She has five adopted children, now between the ages of fourteen and twenty. Yes, that means that at one point she had five teenagers in her house and somehow managed to maintain order—and her sanity. She smiles and laughs easily, while her Hungarian accent enchants the ear.

Her children have spent time in her native Hungary through an exchange program with the Los Angeles chapter of the Hungarian Scout Association. The HSA was formed after the communist government kicked the Scouts out of Hungary. (They've since been welcomed back.) It was at an annual fund-raiser and debutante ball for the Hungarian Scouts that Elizabeth first wore her favorite pair of shoes, a pair of tall black sandals with little diamonds on them. They matched her dress exactly. "The shoes cost me a fortune," says Elizabeth, "but when you step in them you feel like you're walking on a cloud."

Her daughter was one of the debutantes debuting that year. All the girls were required to wear long white dresses and the boys were decked out in their tails and white gloves. She watched as her daughter danced a special waltz each one had to learn. "They practice for months to learn it," explains Elizabeth, who watched very proudly.

Each year the Hungarian Scouts also select an honorary chairperson for this ball, someone who's been heavily involved with the Scouts and contributed a great deal of time and effort to the organization. Given that Elizabeth never goes at anything halfheartedly, it's no surprise that at one of these fund-raisers she was so honored. It's the only other time she's worn her diamond-speckled shoes. "I just don't go to events like that very often," she says.

They introduced Elizabeth by listing all the wonderful things she'd done for the organization, and then they brought out a huge bouquet of flowers for her, along with a gourd that traditionally holds wine. "It's really pretend," she says. "There's really no wine in it, but you're supposed to hold it up and look like you're taking a drink." Her children, dressed in their Scout uniforms, were the ones who brought out the flowers and the gourd. "It was so embarrassing, but I figured I might as well get used to it," she says, with her typical good humor. "It's my day!"

Always one to play her part to the fullest, she then hoisted the gourd to her lips and pretended to take a swig—a very long swig. "My kids said, 'Mom! You held the wine bottle up so long!'" she says and laughs. "It looked like you were really drinking!" She then announced, "Let the ball begin!" and waltzed through that special evening in her shimmering shoes, surrounded by her fortunate children.

There is an art to living that eludes many of us. But not so with Elizabeth, who with her charm and zeal makes preparing a tax return something to look forward to.

N'Orleans Jazz Kicks

King Tut and pneumonia—until Hurricane Katrina hit, these things were what came to mind when I thought of New Orleans. During my only trip there, the town was taken over by a tour of relics from King Tut's tomb. At the same time, I'd brought a case of bronchitis with me, and the shifts between sweltering heat and air-conditioning let pneumonia blossom. After that monstrous hurricane struck, the televised images revived other memories. I glimpsed the street in the French Quarter I toured in a horse-drawn carriage and marveled again at the architecture. I heard that distinctive N'Orleans drawl in an interview and recalled a waiter explaining Cajun cuisine to me. I'd walk out into L.A.'s summer heat and remember the weight of New Orleans's humid air sinking into my pores. Only a storm as big as Katrina could thwart the Big Easy, but its spirit and color remain with all who've known her, however briefly.

MATERIAL LIST

- A pair of dancing shoes
- White acrylic paint (optional)
- Sheet music
- Decorative paper
- Lace
- Crushed velvet
- Trim or cording
- Feathers
- Rhinestones
- Hot glue gun and glue sticks
- White craft glue
- Paintbrush
- Scissors

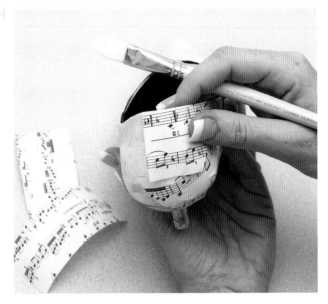

If you're altering a dark pair of shoes, you may want to prime them first with a coat of white acrylic paint (see *Preparing Shoes for Altering*, page 22). Allow the paint to dry, and apply a second coat if necessary for full coverage.

Begin cutting strips of sheet music, and dip them briefly in water. Brush a thin layer of white craft glue onto the shoe where you want to place the sheet music (see *Decoupaging with Paper*, page 25). Shake any excess water off the paper, and position it over the glued area. Mold the paper onto the shoe with your fingertips—thanks to that little swim, the paper should be very pliable. Cover the sheet music with a coat of glue, then continue dipping and gluing until you've covered both shoes. Let your beauties dry.

Pull out the lace, and cut a piece to cover the top panel on the front of a shoe. Decoupage the lace to the surface, and then trim as needed so that it lines up with the shoe's seams (see *Decoupaging with Fabric*, page 27).

Next, cut another piece of lace to drape around the back of the shoe and the heel. Again, brush some glue on the shoe, adhere the lace and then cover the lace with another thin layer of glue.

Pull out the trim and begin edging the shoes with the help of your hot glue gun (see *Adding Trim*, page 28). Add trim around the sole and top edges of the shoes, and also use it to outline the lace panels on the front and back of the shoe. Add an extra line of trim across the heel, just below the sole.

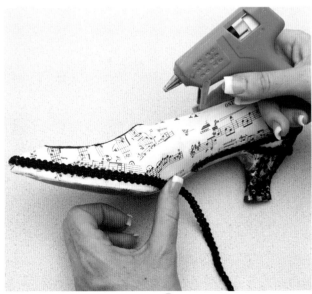

Draw the shape of a small Mardi Gras mask onto the back of the decorative paper. Cut the mask out, and decoupage it on top of the lace at the front of the shoe.

Next, pull out those rhinestones and feathers because it's Mardi Gras time! Festoon the back and front of your shoes with feathers. You need the hot glue gun for this. Make sure you only get glue on the very ends of the feathers or you'll end up with some nasty, gluey clumps.

Finally, use the hot glue gun to add rhinestones at the base of the feathers at the front and back. Cover the entire glued area at the base of the feathers with rhinestones to hide the glue. Remember that space between the 2 lines of trim at the heel? Fill that space with lots and lots of rhinestones. Now you're almost ready for Bourbon Street.

For a final touch, add crushed velvet to the inside of the shoes. Cut a piece of crushed velvet that's approximately the shape of the insole, and use white craft glue to attach it inside the shoe. Line the inner sides of the shoe, as well. In this case, do not cover the velvet with a coat of glue as you normally would with fabric decoupage because it would dull the sheen of the velvet.

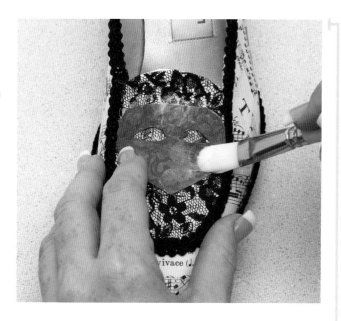

Tips, Tricks & Crazy Things to Try

Feathers are incredibly tricky to work with. They like to shed, clump and break, so be patient with them as well as with yourself while working with them.

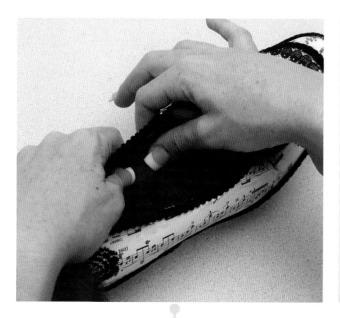

Head over Heels: Shoes with Heart & Sole

ann reed

What Mozart was to music and Shakespeare was to poetry, Ann Harper Reed is to the art of massage. And what she is to massage, she also is to great conversation. There's something transcendent about the talks I have with her, and she's one of the few I'll discuss spirituality with because to me it's such a private and individual experience. The same openness and clarity that come through in her words also make her such an extraordinary massage therapist.

Ann works with the muscles of the human body the way a skilled piano tuner coaxes each key until it resonates as it should. Just as the piano tuner gives each key particular attention, so Ann adjusts her massage technique to suit each client's therapeutic needs. After an hour under her care, backaches evaporate and calmness pervades. Her award-winning aromatherapy line, too, is soothing and different from all the rest.

"When you do massage, you wear practical shoes," she says, since she spends a great deal of time on her feet and needs to maintain leverage and balance when working on clients. But her favorite shoes are "a really beautiful pair of leather shoes," she says, "handmade in Italy." She bought them a few years ago at a little boutique in Old Town Pasadena. Her business was then based there, in a day spa where the owner was proving difficult. "I was trying to make my business work, but I was sacrificing myself left and right," she says. "There was a very clear point in time when the business wasn't going to work the way I wanted it to." That's when she decided to leave and strike out on her own.

The day spa's owner had Dom Perignon tastes, had the money to accommodate those tastes, and spent a lot of her time doing so. Ann, who's quite the opposite in nature, found it interesting to observe. "It was fascinating to explore that," Ann says, "and to see the amount of sadness behind living like that." When Ann decided she was leaving the day spa, she opted to go out shopping with the owner. "I thought it would be interesting to connect with the finer stuff of life," she says, "and then let go."

That's how she found her Italian shoes. "They were outside what I could afford at the time," she says, "but it was a symbolic gesture." And that one gesture was enough. She took her business and moved on. "It was great to move on from all that," she says, "and live the life I wanted to." She very much prefers not having someone else to report to. "I'm not servile to anyone," she states. "That's part of what buying those shoes was about. I feel very much in my own power when I wear them."

Beyond the symbolism, there's also just the way the shoes look and make her feel. "I've worn them any time I want to feel really, really special," she tells me. "They have a very sexy line to them." The leather has a mild metallic sheen mixing gold, bronze and copper hues. "People always say, 'Those are amazing shoes,'" she says. "You can have shorts and a T-shirt on, and then you put them on and you are transformed. You're a movie star." There's one more thing she loves about them. "They came with their own little bag to keep the dust off of them," she says. "I don't have a lot of really nice shoes, so I store them and know that they're safe."

In addition to maintaining her massage business and aromatherapy line, she has also published one amazing novel, *Element of Blank*, and is working on a second. As a result, her vibrant insights now have a wider audience, so more people can benefit from her humanity and attention to detail—not just those of us who need the knots coaxed out of our necks and shoulders.

Fashionista Flip-Flops

Few forms of footwear are quite as easy to get into and out of than flip-flops. No wonder we love them! We all know summer has truly arrived when they emerge from the closet. Though all shoes make a bit of noise as we walk in them, there's nothing quite as distinctive as the rhythmic flapping of these sandals. For a long time, they were only acceptable in casual environments, but if you're a fashionista, don't despair. Now you can deck out these summer classics with trinkets, ribbons and anything else that can be squeezed onto those slim straps.

material LIST
- A pair of flip-flops
- Thick trim or ribbon
- Thin trim or ribbon
- Silk leaves with wire stems
- Buttons
- Rhinestones
- Hot glue gun and glue sticks
- Scissors
- Tweezers or needle-nose pliers

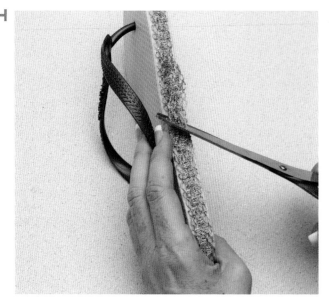

Use the hot glue gun to attach thick trim around the soles of the flip-flops; make sure you press it firmly into place (see *Adding Trim*, page 28). The trim will be very close to the ground when you walk, and you don't want anything sliding or jabbing into your foot.

Fasten the thin trim or ribbon at the base of 1 of the straps with a dot of hot glue, right where the strap emerges from the sole. Begin winding the trim or ribbon around the strap, overlapping it slightly so that none of the strap shows through. Secure the ribbon or trim with hot glue after every few wraps to make sure it will stay in place. Don't forget to wind the trim or ribbon around the center post before continuing on to the other strap. Where the end of the plastic strap is attached to the flip flop, add a big dollop of hot glue, snip the trim or ribbon, and press the end firmly into place.

Next, place a silk leaf against 1 of the straps with the wire end where the straps meet and wrap the wire end completely around the covered strap. To make the leaf more secure, add a dab of glue to the wire as well as under the leaf. Repeat to add a leaf to the other strap.

Glue a button in the middle of the leaves, and glue another button on top of that. Glue rhinestones on top of the buttons. Just paint your toenails, and you're ready for summer!

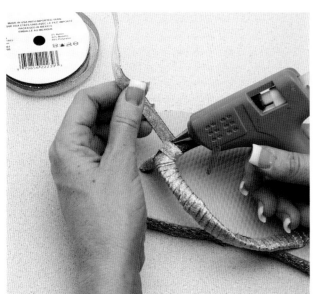

Tips, Tricks & Crazy Things to Try

Unfortunately, adornments sometimes look nicer than they feel. It's important when you create your own pair of flip-flops that you add things that are as kind to the toes as they are to the eyes.

Head over Heels: Shoes with Heart & Sole

Marcia Parisi

In February 2005, Marcia Parisi sprinkled fairy dust on me. My handcrafted jewelry business was still very new, and I'd gone to the Craft & Hobby Association's huge trade show in hopes of learning more about the business and making a contact or two. At one point amid the miles of aisles and thousands of vendors, I was standing in a crowd outside a book publisher's booth, looking to pick up a catalog and maybe someone's business card. I knew I wasn't yet sufficiently established as a designer to approach any publishers about writing or contributing to a book, but I hoped that perhaps in three to five years I might be able to get someone to hear me out.

"I can tell you a little about this," a woman to my left said, "if you're curious." I turned to see if she was talking to me. Fortunately, she was, and that's how I met Marcia, who conveniently worked for the publisher. Conversing with her was as effortless as breathing. Within a half hour, she had introduced me to key players from her company. When I followed up with her a week later, she asked if I wanted to contribute a few designs to a new book they were doing. Within a month, I also had a deal in place for a book of original jewelry designs.

Fairy dust, I'm telling you.

That publisher went belly-up several months later, but, miraculously, those books survived. Even before that company folded, Marcia had elected to return to her former career working with a home care and hospice agency for which she does community outreach. I know from experiencing her wide-open heart that the people talking with Marcia about hospice care must feel so relieved after she's explained things to them. It's so difficult to begin those conversations, and things so often and so easily become clumsy or disconnected. Marcia's gift to the world is that she's willing to be a confident advocate for others, whether she's dealing with a person in need of in-home rehab or with a jumpy would-be author.

With Marcia's down-to-earth nature, it's no surprise that the Birkenstocks she bought during her first year in college in 1973 remain her favorite shoes. "The whole heel bed is gone," she laughs. "I've worn them so much I've worn away the back of them." They still have the two thick dark beige straps in front, though. She got teased a lot in school because her comfortable sandals weren't the most attractive footwear. "I'd just tell people I'm a college student," she says, "and I'm doing more walking than riding."

Marcia wore those shoes all through college. After she graduated, they went with her when she visited a friend working for the Peace Corps in Africa. "They're very well traveled shoes," she says, listing Malawi, Mozambique, Tanzania, Kenya and South Africa as places she's trekked through while wearing them. After Africa, she was off to Europe for a month and a half. "My sandals got to go back home," she tells me, "because we went to Germany," which is where Birkenstocks are made. "They got to see their homeland," she says and laughs. "Shoes should know their roots." Despite the fact that from the middle of the sole backward there's not much shoe left, she can't let them go. "Every time I think of throwing them away, I can't," she says. "There's just too much sentimental value."

When Marcia gets attached to someone or something, it's sure to be well taken care of. How lucky was I to be standing in that place at the moment when Marcia happened to be next to me? How big is the night sky? How deep are the oceans? That's how lucky I was, and that's because her compassion and generosity are so boundless that every chat with Marcia beats any gift a fairy godmother ever bestowed with a magic wand.

Santa Baby Stilettos

How I love the color red! It's bold, it stirs the blood, and it goes great with my complexion. Green is also a cheery, flattering color at the holidays, and it symbolizes so many wonderful things like life, love and happiness. But I'll take crimson, scarlet and all of red's other permutations. I like red with hints of blue as well as red tinged with sunset orange. I can't stand the taste of red wine, but I do love the color! It's vibrant and passionate. It reminds me of the Christmases I spent in Mexico when I was doing human rights work. There was the red in Mexican art, in the terra-cotta pots and in nature itself. The chilies were magnificent to look at, though I didn't dare eat them. Red—so powerful, so evocative, and so very irresistible.

material LIST

- A pair of stilettos
- Miniature round Christmas ornaments
- Floral Christmas decorations
- Hot glue gun and glue sticks
- Scissors
- Tweezers or needle-nose pliers

My floral decorations were too big to use as-is, so I separated all of the components in order to use the pieces I wanted. These decorations yielded leaf layers and beaded clusters. You never know what you'll discover when you take things apart—but first you have to fight that voice that says, "You can't do that!" Don't be afraid to take apart a decoration and see what it's made of. Once you deconstruct the decorations, you're ready to go.

Use a hot glue gun to spread glue across the front straps of the shoe. Carefully attach a piece of floral decoration to the front of the shoe. Add some hot glue on top of that, and press a second layer into position. Place this layer at an angle, so the top layer alternates with the layer below.

Next, pull off the caps used to hang the ornaments. Add a dab of glue at the center of the leaves, and press an ornament into the glue. Arrange 3 more ornaments to form a cluster, and glue them into place, as well. Make sure to lay the ornaments on their sides so that they'll lie flat.

Aim some hot glue directly into the center of the ornament cluster, and push one of the beaded clusters from the floral decorations into the glue.

Attach 1 layer of leaves to the back of the heel. Next, snip 5–6 of the beads from the beaded clusters. Add some hot glue to the center of the leaves on the heel. Use tweezers or needle-nose pliers to carefully place the beads into the glue to form a circle. Let all of the glue dry, and you're ready to kick up your heels at the office Christmas party.

Tips, Tricks & Crazy Things to Try

Christmas ornaments can be fragile, so make sure you don't have a clumsy dance partner, or you could end up with shattered shoes!

Head over Heels: Shoes with Heart & Sole

SHERENE HULUGALLE

Like all the organically grown flowers in Sherene Hulugalle's Wisteria Lane Flower Shop, the roses are colorful, voluptuous and as abundant as Sherene's laughter. You'd think from her enchanting way with customers that her life's been carefree. She laughs when she calls herself "a human rights junkie," but Sherene's is one of the truest hearts I've ever known.

Sherene grew up in Kandy, a small town in the central province of Sri Lanka, where the human rights situation is a vicious one. The government is bad enough. That the rebel group the Tamil Tigers can be just as violent makes it agonizing. So whom do you support if, like Sherene, you care more about people's well-being than political power? "I was on the side of anyone being abused," she says, "especially the women and children, who always seem to suffer the worst from all sides."

This meant, unfortunately, that Sherene and her sister wound up on the enemy lists of both factions and, therefore, in twice the danger. "My mother never wanted both of us to go to vote together," Sherene says with her musical accent. "She didn't tell us not to vote. She'd just say, 'Please go separately so that one of you will come back,' because she wanted at least one daughter alive." Sherene then chuckles and adds, "She didn't care which one."

Her mother set an example for her daughters by opening a shelter for pregnant rape victims, who are considered a shame to their families. The shelter is a safe place for them to have their babies and also to learn a trade so they can support themselves. Sherene's mother also tries to reunite these women with their families. "My mother works on the mothers of these girls," Sherene explains, "and basically makes them take back their daughters."

But Sherene's father, a botanist and landscape architect, instilled her love of the beauty nature produces. He's also the one who gave Sherene her favorite pair of shoes following a business trip to Japan in 1978. The three-inch platform geisha shoes with a vinyl strap across the top were ceremonial, not practical, and meant for illusion rather than the reality of Sri Lankan roads and typical teenage vanity.

Sherene wore those blazing red platforms everywhere. "I was sure I was the hottest girl in town! No one had platform shoes like that," she says and laughs. "Looking back now, I'm mortified. My friends were so jealous. They were all rich, they could have everything—but they couldn't get these shoes!" She'd strut, not walk, up and down the streets of Kandy (population ten thousand) for no reason but to show off her red shoes. "I wore them until my feet outgrew them," she says, "until the heel of my foot was sticking out the back. Probably about a year, because I was growing so fast. That was a good year!" What a figure she must have struck, a twelve-year-old girl with limbs lean as flower stems parading all around Kandy atop those siren-red wedges.

"Now I dress in black," says this mother of two. "It's easy, and everything matches! But I still have a thing about red shoes." More waves of delightful laughter. "But I've never had anything as hot as those red platforms. That was the pinnacle!"

Her bouquets now do the showing off in their organic, chemical-free way. Sherene's humanitarian side is still alive and well in other ways, too. She works with a number of organizations but now does it here, where she can raise her children more safely.

She still manages to visit her family in Sri Lanka but has to be careful. "My brother says when you've ticked off everyone," she says, "you've obviously got it right or very, very wrong." As difficult and dangerous as things have been for her at times, her reward is seeing beauty and mystery in everyday things, whether they're as tiny as a tea rose or as tall as those platform shoes.

Strollin' Down the Aisle Pumps

Granted, a bride probably would want everyone to be enraptured by her glowing face rather than by her footwear. But, if you plan on having your groom toss your garter at the reception, wearing shoes that will impress your guests is not a bad idea. Even if that's not the case, having a little shimmer on your shoes will only enhance your overall sparkle. And it's not a bad idea to add some dazzle to your bridesmaids' footwear, too, since the idea of dyed to match makes everyone secretly moan. Why not host a shoe party and make your shoes together? Then your bridesmaids might actually wear their shoes again. Take it from one who was a bridesmaid many, many times: I loved all the weddings, but the shoes were rock-bottom hopeless! A little redesign can go a very long way in this case, both for the bride and for her best friends.

material List

- A pair of high-heeled bridal shoes
- Lace
- Rhinestones
- Small floral wedding decorations
- Hot glue gun and glue sticks
- White craft glue
- Paintbrush
- Scissors
- Wire cutters
- Tweezers or needle-nose pliers

Separate the floral decorations into individual stems. Using wire cutters and scissors, deconstruct 4 stems (or more, if you choose) for each shoe, separating the flowers, stems and leaves. Use a hot glue gun to glue 2 leaves to the front of each shoe, then arrange 4 flowers on top of each set of leaves and attach them as well. To surround this group of flowers with some delicate sparkle, use tweezers or needle-nose pliers and a hot glue gun to glue 3 small rhinestones on both sides of each arrangement.

Gather 4–6 complete flowers together to form a bouquet, making sure that they're arranged nicely. I streamlined my bouquet by removing several excess leaves, which you may want to do as well. Clip all the stems to a uniform length with wire cutters. Hold the bouquet in the middle, and use a hot glue gun to apply glue to the stems from just below your fingertips to the ends to hold the bouquet together. Let the glue cool and harden, then glue the flowers to the outside of the shoes with a hot glue gun, positioning the bouquet so that the buds aim toward the heel.

Cut a triangle-shaped piece of lace that is long enough to cover the stems of the bouquet. Using a hot glue gun, glue one side of the triangle alongside the bouquet. Wrap the lace around the flowers and glue it to the shoe along the other side of the bouquet, making sure to tuck the lace edge underneath as you attach it so it won't unravel. Use a paintbrush to coat the lace with white craft glue to stiffen it and keep it from shifting.

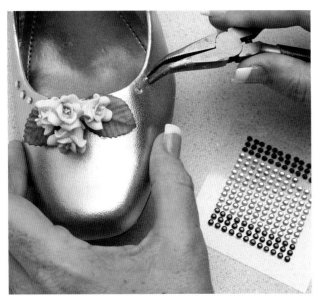

Tips, Tricks & Crazy Things to Try

Start by deconstructing one decoration to see how many parts it has. The more parts there are, the more you'll have to play with. Experiment with a few different kinds of decorations before committing to a design.

Head over Heels: Shoes with Heart & Sole

MELONIE JOHNSON

When the office air-conditioning conks out or when a stream of rainwater starts running down the conference room wall, it's a building's property manager who gets the call. If there's a company moving in or moving out, the property manager supervises the comings and goings. And that's just the tip of the commercial iceberg when it comes to operating the tall structures that form our cities' skylines. Melonie Johnson is the one in charge of a few hundred thousand square feet of prime office space in west Los Angeles, which means she's the one who gets the call whenever there's a problem, day or night, weekday or holiday.

It's difficult being a businesswoman, and we all need to unleash some steam once in a while. Melonie's one of the people I can do that with. Maybe it's because we laugh at any and every opportunity or because we each have strong opinions and just adore sharing them, whether you want us to or not. Then again, she does love chocolate cake as much as I do. Whatever the reason, it's always a hoot to sit down and get a little silly with her.

The last time I walked into Melonie's office, I noticed she was rubbing her face with her hand as we spoke, but that was all I saw until she gave me a one-finger salute with the ring finger of her left hand. "You're engaged!" I said, finally seeing the bright bauble on her finger. She and her fiancé had met four years prior at a poker game. Melonie's smart and, unlike a lot of women, has the confidence to kick to the curb anyone who doesn't treat her well. This one, as it turned out, was a keeper.

Melonie's always been athletic, and she has a wonderful competitive spirit. But once she met her man, "We spent most of our time going to restaurants and snuggling on the couch," she says. "All the activities went by the wayside." In two years, she says she gained fifty pounds. (It didn't look that way to me, but I'm notorious for being oblivious to things like weight—and engagement rings, apparently.)

Once they settled on a wedding date, Melonie's favorite pair of shoes became her new pair of running sneakers. "I decided I didn't want to be so heavy in our wedding pictures," she says. "Those pictures will follow us through our lifetime, and I just don't feel that's who I am." So she joined an exercise program and in only two months dropped half the weight she'd gained. She won't quit until she's back in full fighting trim, right in time for her upcoming nuptials.

In addition to the metallic turquoise stripes along the sides—"I'm in a turquoise/aqua phase right now"—her otherwise white sneakers have good support and cushioning, "which helps me stay injury free while running," she says. "I'm having such a great time trying to force my nearly forty-year-old body to do things I haven't done in years. It gives me a sense of freedom." Her robust return to form "has made me feel like a kid again," she adds.

She does it all in spite of her asthma—and because there's a history of obesity in her family. Her own mother even told her, "It's just easier to be fat," a sentiment thankfully not shared by Melonie. "I feel like I have control over my destiny with my running shoes. I am persisting, driving, and working hard to be who I want to be—fun, fit, happy and successful."

I'm sure it's also made racing between building floors easier when the power goes out. Melonie's been told she fits into the "expressive" personality category. This enthusiasm and verve endear her to her friends and make her great at keeping the companies residing in her buildings content to stay where they are. And in Los Angeles real estate, that's a trick.

Seashell Sandals

Is there anyone who's visited the seashore and not collected seashells? I suppose there are those who prefer to spend all afternoon in the water or snoozing in the sun, but to me beachcombing is like digging for buried treasure. I've been teased by my sun-loving companions for spending all day stooped over with my nails raking the sand. Then they spend the whole ride home admiring my exquisite finds. Shells, after all, were humankind's first embellishment. The oldest piece of jewelry still in existence is a necklace made of a delicate string of shells. So, given that I was an ancient history major, I thought it only appropriate to include a time-honored decoration in one of my designs. Since I live in southern California, I have plenty of beach close at hand.

material LIST
- A pair of sandals
- Lace
- Ribbon or trim
- Seashells
- Tissue paper
- Hot glue gun and glue sticks
- White craft glue
- Tissue paper
- Paintbrush
- Scissors

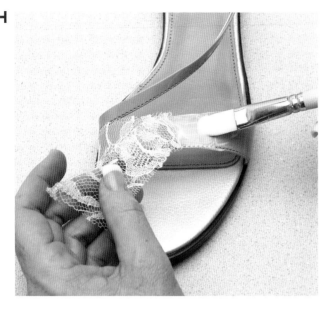

Create tissue paper patterns for the heel of the sandals as well as the front strap (see *Creating a Pattern*, page 24). Use these patterns to cut out pieces of lace; be careful not to snag the material on your scissors—or anything else pointy!

Brush a layer of white craft glue onto the heel, and glue the lace into position (see *Decoupaging with Fabric*, page 27). Add a thin coat of glue over the top of the lace to seal it. This will make the lace sturdier and keep it clean. Do the same to add lace to the front strap. Set the sandals aside until they've dried thoroughly.

Next, use the hot glue gun to add ribbon or trim along all the edges of the lace (see *Adding Trim*, page 28). The ribbon will create a neat border. Add ribbon or trim to any additional straps, but do not cover any buckle holes in the straps.

Arrange the shells before adding them to the sandals. Then, use small dabs from the hot glue gun to add the shell design to the top of each front strap. Once all the shells are glued in place, brush on a coat of white craft glue to seal the shells and to give them an attractive topcoat.

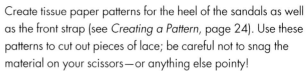

Tips, Tricks & Crazy Things to Try

The next time you're at the beach, try sifting through the sand for small shells to use for this project. You'll probably find more than you need, and your new decorations will carry good memories, too.

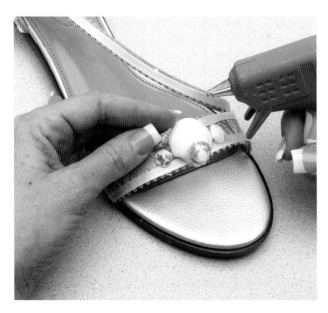

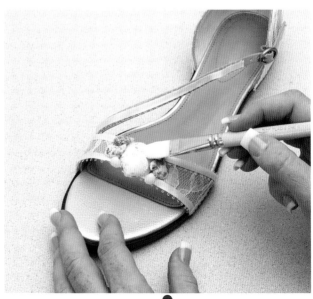

Head over Heels: Shoes with Heart & Sole

Jeanne Lusignan

For someone who knows so much about myths and fairy tales, it's remarkable how grounded in reality Jeanne Lusignan is. We were schoolmates more than twenty years ago and knew one another well then. But after school we'd only occasionally see each other—a party here, a barbeque there, that sort of thing.

Then, three years ago, Jeanne sent me an e-mail, and I wish I could remember the exact words she wrote. As dreadful as the message was, Jeanne's words were straightforward, along the lines of, "There's no simple or easy way to tell you this, so I'll just say it. I have breast cancer." Because my mother had died from colon cancer while Jeanne and I were in graduate school, there was much to talk about. Granted, those cancers are very different, but the experience of facing death is not. I respected the way Jeanne refused to shy away from her odds. In fact, she embraced them and endeavored to improve them in every way she could. When she read that women who walked a half hour every day improved their chances of survival by fifty percent, she walked every single day, even to her chemotherapy sessions. "I made myself walk no matter how sick I was," she says.

That Christmas, she and her husband, Jaime, were driving from California to Oregon to spend the holidays with her family. "I was still very sick and I was bald," she says, "and I was cold because I was bald." She wore turbans and hats in bright colors to keep warm. She'd made many of them herself, seeing as she's quite a sewer—as well as a writer, designer and accomplished artist. Each day, Jeanne and Jaime drove only for as long as Jeanne could handle it, and then they'd stop at a hotel. She still walked a half hour every day, wherever they were.

The township of Willits rests up in the mountains of northern California. "It's a beautiful little town," says Jeanne, "that's a throwback to the hippie era with all these great little stores." She noticed that there were a number of hospices there amid the crags and peaks. "Jaime and I kind of discussed that this would be a nice place to come," she says, "if I had to." She chose to do her daily walk there, looking in the shop windows with Jaime beside her. A tall pair of slippers caught her eye. "They were red and black with flowers on them. They looked Chinese," she says. "They were meant to look like cowboy boots, but the shape of them was straight out of a kung fu movie." They were lined with faux fur and were rather expensive, especially for slippers. "But I really wanted them," she says, "and Jaime said, 'Why don't you get them?'" So they became an early Christmas gift. "I wore them the whole rest of the trip because they were comfy and warm," she tells me, "and I could curl up in the car."

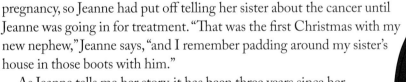

When they arrived in Oregon, Jeanne met her sister Annie's son for the first time. Annie had had a difficult pregnancy, so Jeanne had put off telling her sister about the cancer until Jeanne was going in for treatment. "That was the first Christmas with my new nephew," Jeanne says, "and I remember padding around my sister's house in those boots with him."

As Jeanne tells me her story, it has been three years since her diagnosis. Her hair's grown back, and her design eye is as finely honed as ever. She tires more easily, though, and it's too early to say she's in remission. But she's working—with me, for which I'm fortunate—and remains the steady influence she's always been. The slippers from that lovely place in the mountains also remain. "I wear them all the time," Jeanne says.

This may not be the gleeful and uncluttered ending one finds in a fairy tale, but it is one of Jeanne's own making—and, really, it's not yet an ending at all.

Safari Sneakers

On the store shelf these sneakers looked so hideous that I couldn't resist the challenge. The photos I decoupaged on them are from a safari I went on with my father shortly after my mother died. I know from my journals that my mood and his ranged from miserable to distant to downright obnoxious as we struggled to deal with my mother's passing. However, what I remember most now are all the extraordinary creatures we watched from the air as well as the ground, thanks to an unforgettable hot-air balloon ride that I had to convince my father to take. Ironic, since I'm the one with a fear of heights and he's the former hotshot fighter pilot. I recall rising with the sun as it crept over the Serengeti's horizon and sensing that this trip was one of my mother's final gifts to me, so that I might know the world, my father and myself better.

material LIST
- A pair of high-top sneakers
- White acrylic paint (optional)
- Acrylic paint
- Photos from a favorite trip
- Maps, tickets and old passport pages from that trip
- Leather trim
- Hot glue gun and glue sticks
- White craft glue
- Newspaper
- Paintbrush
- Scissors

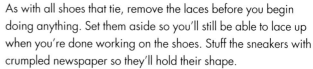

As with all shoes that tie, remove the laces before you begin doing anything. Set them aside so you'll still be able to lace up when you're done working on the shoes. Stuff the sneakers with crumpled newspaper so they'll hold their shape.

Collect your maps, old passport pages, and travel photos together and sort through them. I've found that maps and old passport pages are great for the background, while favorite photos really stand out on top of the maps and passport pages. Make sure any passport pages you use have neither identifying numbers nor unexpired visas, just to be safe.

Scan and print copies of the photos, maps and passport pages so you'll still have the originals. If you'd prefer, you can go to your nearest copy center and simply make color copies.

Now it's time to figure out the layout for your design. Spread all your images on a tabletop and start moving them around. First think about which pieces you'll use to fill in the background, then decide which photos should go where. Trim the photos so that they'll have more of a visual "pop" against the background. Take your time planning your arrangement, and don't be surprised if you change your mind a few times. You can also try taping the images onto your shoes temporarily until you're happy with your design.

If you're altering a dark pair of shoes, you may want to prime them with a coat of white acrylic paint (see *Preparing Shoes for Altering*, page 22). Allow the paint to dry and apply a second coat if necessary for full coverage. Canvas soaks up a lot of paint, so additional layers may be necessary.

Once the paint has dried, glue on the background pieces. Decoupage the papers to the shoe (see *Decoupaging with Paper*, page 25). Make sure there's no sneaker peeking out from underneath your background pieces.

Once your background is complete, begin gluing the photos on top. I added a layer of images while the background pieces were still damp because it made it easier to shape them to the

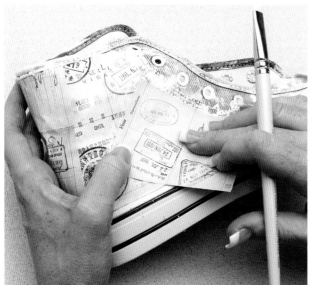

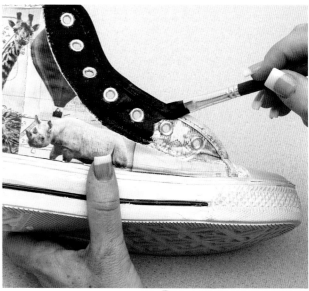

shoe and I didn't have to use as much glue to make them stick. But do be careful as you handle everything so you don't tear any of the paper images, which will be more fragile when they're damp.

Once you've got everything glued down, color in the area around the shoelace holes with the acrylic paint (see *Painting*, page 23). Once this area's dry, brush a coat of white craft glue over the entire sneaker to protect your design from the elements. Set the sneakers aside until they've dried completely. Because high-top sneakers are generally made of canvas, they often take an extra amount of time to dry completely. As anxious as you may be to wear them, please be patient. You're using paper to design this project, and that paper can tear if it's still damp with glue.

Next, get your hot glue gun ready to go and begin adding leather trim all around the edges of the shoe, including the top where your foot slides in (see *Adding Trim*, page 28). Adding all this trim adds color contrast, disguises any rough edges and gives your sneakers a more finished look. Touch up with a bit of acrylic paint any areas on the soles that got messy. Once the paint has dried completely, lace up your shoes and strike out on your next adventure.

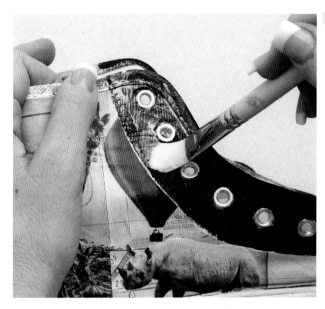

Tips, Tricks & Crazy Things to Try

You can just as easily commemorate a party as a trip with this project. Just substitute pictures of people for the animal photos and use copies of the invitations for the background.

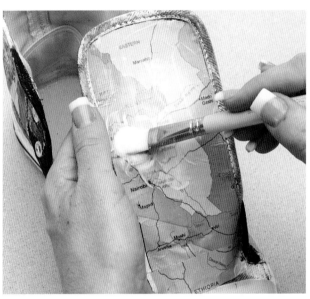

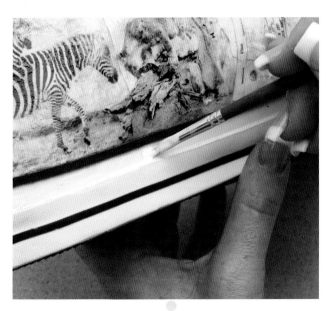

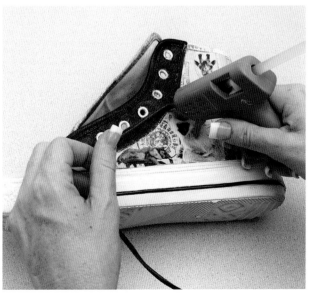

Head over Heels: Shoes with Heart & Sole

Marty Stevens-Heebner

Feet, and therefore shoes, take us on our journey through this land called life. They strut through parties with us and stroll us down the aisle during rituals joyful and sad. They accompany us on our travels to vacation sites or danger spots and carry us to comfort when we need it. Granted, it's easy to scoff at Imelda Marcos's collection or laugh along with *Sex and the City* when Carrie Bradshaw's taken to task for her footwear obsession. But consider the shoe tales told by the women in this book, like the one about Jeanne Lusignan's slippers on page 119 or the shoes Karen Soucy inherited from her mother on page 58, and you can see where shoes become more life support than luxury.

My jungle boots served that way for me when I was doing humanitarian work in Chiapas, Mexico, in the aftermath of the Zapatista rebellion. I had traveled to every continent by late 1994 but had never set foot in Mexico, despite living next door in California. What led me down there? For the sake of brevity, call it a strange series of coincidences. That I became so involved in it all baffled everyone, including me at times. I spoke no Spanish when I first went there and knew little of Mexican history and politics, but from the way the place, the people and the situation beckoned to me I knew this was a byway I needed to explore. Given that the experience provided a clarity and balance I was lacking and transformed every aspect of my life in doing so, it's a good thing I hopped on a plane when I did.

For those of you who are unfamiliar with the lands *sud de la frontera*, Chiapas is the southernmost state of the United States of Mexico (yes, that's its official name), and it borders on Guatemala, which means the coffee grown there is spectacular, as are the revolts. My beige suede jungle boots arrived with me during my first delegation in November 1994 and got me to the airport in time to elude deportation in January 1997. I wasn't in Chiapas the entire time, mind you. I came and went several times and did support work in Los Angeles when I was home.

But those boots got me safely out of the tiny town of Altamirano after I'd been followed by *federales* all day and out of trouble a few months later when two hundred angry villagers surrounded our van. My jungle boots held my feet steady even as my limbs shook at roadblocks manned by machine gun-toting soldiers, and then my boots helped me deliver antibiotics to isolated villages and letters to nuns at remote hospitals. They walked me out of a wrecked bus moments after we narrowly avoided plunging down a fifty foot concrete escarpment when the brakes gave out. They also got stuck in the mud amid the latrines inside Zapatista territory and kept my feet dry when the rains deluged the cobblestone streets of San Cristobal de las Casas, the colonial town I was based in.

Those boots also played a part in a few romances, though I'll spare you the details. I've told those close to me that I don't think I fully came into womanhood until my time in Mexico. I don't mean that in a coy or titillating way. Rather, in Mexico my unrestrained personality was welcomed instead of ridiculed, and for the first time, I felt attractive just being myself, with my persona unaltered and unadorned.

The soles of those boots are worn smooth now from all the miles I put on them, and I haven't donned them in several years. Though they live in the back of my closet now, they are never forgotten. They carried me through such a vital part of my life and were with me when I faced and overcame so much fear. To ever let them go would be like giving away not only those memories but also the wisdom wrung from them. As silly as it sounds, there's too much soul in those soles for me to ever part with my jungle boots.

Resources

There are so many great sources for supplies and inspiration to suit all of your crafting needs. Here are just a few of my favorite resources for ideas and materials.

Supplies

Beacon Adhesives
www.beacon1.com
Fabri-Tac permanent adhesive

Best-Test
www.papercement.com
Rubber cement

Caldex Enterprises
www.oldworldart.com
Gilding supplies

Creative Papers Online
handmade-paper.us
Unique handmade paper

Delta Creative
www.deltacreative.com
Delta Dreamcoat acrylic paint

Eberhard Faber
www.fimo.com
Polymer clay

Elmer's
www.elmers.com
Rubber cement, white craft glue

Krylon
www.krylon.com
Spray paint

Marvy Uchida
www.marvy.com
Fabric markers

Plaid
www.plaidonline.com
Mod Podge, Apple Barrel Colors acrylic paint

For all things ghoulish:
www.halloweentownstore.com

For a list of spectacular bead shows:
www.intergem.com
www.gemfaire.com

Inspiration

Blogs
Jenny Doh, editor in chief of over thirty magazines, including *Somerset Studio* and *Belle Armoire*
www.jennydoh.typepad.com

Jennifer Perkins, owner of the Naughty Secretary Club and host of the DIY Network's *Craft Lab* and *Stylelicious*
naughtysecretaryclub.blogspot.com

Magazines
Belle Armoire
Altered Couture
Somerset Studio
Stampington Inspirations
The Stampers' Sampler
To find stores carrying these magazines, go to *www.stampington.com*.

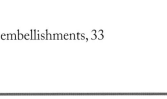

Altered Style
Sewing & Embellishing
Wearable Fashions
Stephanie Kimura
Learn how to create new garments
and goodies by altering items you
already own. Transform a worn
pair of jeans into a skirt or a bag,
and open a whole new world of
wardrobe opportunities.
ISBN 10: 0-89689-600-5
ISBN 13: 978-0-89689-600-0
paperback
8¼" × 10⅞"
128 pages
Z1658

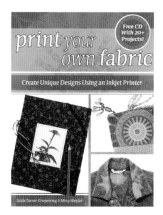

Print Your Own Fabric
Create Unique Designs
Using an Inkjet Printer
Linda Turner Griepentrog
and Missy Shepler
Create your own fabrics using 20
ready-to-print images and instructions
explained in this book/CD package.
Projects include pillows, quilts, bags,
journals and totes.
ISBN 10: 0-89689-247-6
ISBN 13: 978-0-89689-247-7
paperback
8¼" × 10⅞"
144 pages
IJFP

AlterNation
Transform. Embellish. Customize.
Shannon Okey and
Alexandra Underhill
This is the indie-crafter's DIY fashion
bible to personalizing wardrobes
with a wide range of no-sew and
low-sew techniques.
ISBN 10: 1-58180-978-6
ISBN 13: 978-1-58180-978-7
paperback
8" × 10"
144 pages
Z0713

My Style, My Place
Allyce King and Nicole Thieret
Empower a young sewing sister
to tap into her own individualistic
and creative spirit and explore the
possibilities of 25 quick do-it-yourself
projects for the home and wardrobe.
ISBN 10: 0-89689-538-6
ISBN 13: 978-0-89689-538-6
paperback
8¼" × 10⅞"
128 pages
Z0935

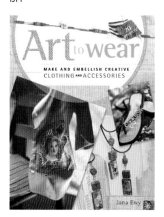

Art to Wear
Jana Ewy
Readers will learn how to create
unique accessories with a wide
range of popular crafting techniques.
It's quick, easy fun with 20 projects
that dress up everything from jewelry
and purses to belts and shoes.
ISBN 10: 1-58180-597-7
ISBN 13: 978-1-58180-597-0
paperback
8½" × 11"
96 pages
33110

These and other fine Krause Publications craft
books are available at your local art & craft
retailer, bookstore or online supplier or visit our
web site at **www.mycraftivity.com**.